Readers Respond

What a delight it was to be reminded of everyday life in the 50's and 60's in a farming community. Maybe it DOESN'T require a "village" to raise a child ... a township seems to have done the job just fine in the case of the Porter children. The contributions of extended family, neighbors, churches, teachers, doctors and friends were shown to be the treasures that they truly are in this down-to-earth memoir. I wish the children of today could experience the life of hard work, self-esteem, generosity, faith, respect and love that I read on these pages.

A Reader

I enjoyed reading your book very much. I grew up in a farming community, but I never understood what farming was really like. Through your use of simple anecdotes, I became a part of your family—sharing in the joys, challenges, and the crises that come your way. I never had really appreciated the sacrifices and rewards of farming until I read this book. It was both nostalgic and educational.

I, of course, could most identify with your chapter on our church. That was a nice tribute you gave Dad. They were great years.

Paul Adams

We have both read your book and enjoyed it very much. You did an excellent job of research, organizing and writing.

Fred and Fran Bartlett

Your book tells what "family farm" will always mean to me. The work of all the members of the family, the integration of the family into the community, and the bonds with neighbors and extended family is the heart and soul of the good life we were able to experience growing up in this setting. I'm so glad to have shared the life depicted in your book. I'm delighted that you've been able to share this with so many.

Ann Pratt Scott

Your book tells a great story, very special to me as my own early life in New Hampshire so closely parallels yours. It took me much longer to read than would normally be the case as every few paragraphs recalled similar memories of my own experiences—things that I had forgotten or not recalled for many, many years.

I wanted to let you know that there are benefits to writing this type of family history beyond those to your family and to your Michigan neighbors. Thanks for the memories that were rediscovered.

Jack Smith

I was raised on a farm in South Dakota and everything I read took me home. What fun! You brought back so many great memories. I think being a farm kid was the best way in the world to grow up. Thank you for the trip down memory lane.

Wanda Oleson Holman

How easy it is to forget where we came from and what shaped our lives. Phyllis Dolislager plows up the fields of the past and germinates in our minds and hearts the roots of upbringing and the effect it has on our lives. For so many, a life in touch with "the ground" that moved slow enough to influence an individual has eluded us. Read this and count yourself enriched or cheated . . . depending on your upbringing. Use the lessons to instill in your present life and the lives of those you are responsible for ways to realign with meaning.

Dave Kendall

Your Aunt Dee gave me your book, and I really enjoyed it. I can relate to most of it as my grandparents lived on a farm in Traverse City. They had an outhouse also, but it was only a two-seater. I remember it most when it was -20 degrees, and you had to go out there before going to bed. I also enjoyed reading about the different people in your book. Being from Rockford, I knew most of them.

Gary Edgecomb

Your book sure brought back a lot of memories. Your college age class at Oakfield was the first Sunday School class I'd ever taught. You guys had a lot of patience with me. Like the time the lesson was on "Matters for the Married." My comment was, "None of you are married, so we'll skip that lesson." You and the class taught me a lesson that day when you insisted that I needed to teach it because you had plans to get married. Thank you for sharing your memories and talents with us.

Frank Austin

What a fun excursion into my past. When my daughter comes home I will let her read your book if she wants a picture of what life was like for me growing up in Michigan.

When I go back to Rockford and people get excited about going to the Old Mill it is funny to me. I never would have dreamed that would attract people from all over Michigan. My memories were backing up to the loading dock and leaving the pickup there while Mom and I hurried all over town doing errands so we would be back to take the load of feed home after it was ground.

You didn't mention learning to drive. The hay fields were the training grounds for all of us. I must have been about six when Dad put me on the tractor and told me to steer between the bales while they picked up the hay. The pedals were so stiff and I was so small, I couldn't push them. If I had to stop, someone would run up and hop on behind me and push in the pedals. Later, when I was a bit older, I would grab the steering wheel, stand up on the pedals and pull against the steering wheel with all my might to force the pedals down.

I just had to take a minute and thank you for the fun your book brought. I read every line and every appendix entry and knew how very real it all was. You did a wonderful job!

Carol Erhart Morrill

I really enjoyed reading the farm book. I devoured it in a short time, and it was great. I could identify with so much in the book. I loved every page, including your mother's columns and the diary, the black and white floor, young people's group, church twice on Sundays and Wednesdays, and more items too numerous to relate.

Suzanne Kavgian

Books by

Phyllis Porter Dolislager

Moved Out of Our Comfort Zone (2007)
We moved . . . three times in twelve months!

Simple Ways to Share Your Faith (2006)
Pointing People to Jesus

I Pray for You on Wednesday (2004)
How to Energize Your God-Time

The Missing Part of Your Will: Your Testament (2004)
How to Write an Ethical Will

Good Morning . . . Let the Stress Begin (2003, 2005, 2006)
and other writings to encourage you to publish your stories

A King-Size Bed, A Silk Tree, and a Fry Pan (2003)
and other stories of Faith, Family & Friendship

Lessons Learned on the Farm (2001, 2007)
A Step Back in Time when Life was Simpler
And Family was Celebrated

Lessons Learned on the Farm

A Step Back in Time When Life Was Simpler and Family Was Celebrated

Phyllis Porter Dolislager

Eleanor Porter Grifhorst, Ronald Porter, Charles Porter,
Darcia Porter Kelley

xulon PRESS

Dedication

In memory of our father, Darcy Porter, whose vision and work
ethic truly made him a successful farmer

For our Mother, Eleanor Porter Grifhorst, who joined hands with
Dad and shared his vision

For our spouses, children, and grandchildren, may you gain a
perspective of our farm heritage

For the many hands and lives that touched us on the farm,
thank you

For the real, unsung heroes: America's farmers

Preface

You don't have to be a millionaire to leave a legacy.

Growing up on a farm didn't seem particularly special to any of us. We grumbled and complained like all kids about the chores that we did and because we always had to get home to milk the cows. But we accepted it; it was our way of life. We never did understand why our city cousins and friends thought it was so great.

Now that we're adults with children and grandchildren of our own, we think it was the best thing that ever happened to us. The farm was the perfect training ground for learning the traits of success. Our parents truly were role models for us. The work was hard and getting it done right the first time was important. We didn't waste time.

The routine of farm living taught us discipline. There was work to be done and we did it: hay to be brought into the barn, cows to milk, crops to plant, trips to make to pick up parts for a break-down, calves to feed. We saw our work yield rewards. We saw the haymow fill up. We saw the milk level in the bulk tank increase. We saw the wheat harvested and sold. We saw broken implements fixed. We saw calves grow and get moved to different pens.

Dad and Mother were ahead of their time in giving psychological rewards too. We were told that we had worked hard or had done a good job. We were given thank you's. Whether it was picking green beans in the garden or throwing off a wagonload of hay, we knew we were appreciated.

Spiritual discipline was another large part of our lives. We had family devotions without fail. We heard our parents pray out loud. We saw Dad pray before he bought a new implement or cattle. We knew that Dad read his Bible at 3:30 a.m. before going out to milk the cows at 4:00 a.m. We saw Mother care for others less fortunate. Regularly we saw her show hospitality in our house. Our friends were always welcome, and she invited people who were role models for us. Often we had missionaries and pastors in our home.

Believing that there are valuable lessons of life and faith to be gained by examining our past, and that family history is important because the family is the fundamental unit of society, we have recorded a small portion of our family's unique heritage of not only living on a dairy farm, but prospering as well. We learned that persistence is the face of success. We learned that hard work and integrity go hand in hand. We learned that relationships and working together paid dividends.

What we wouldn't give to be able to spend one more day at the farm with Dad and Mother and each other. But that's not possible. What is possible is to record our memories in the hopes that a few of the lessons we learned and the values we gained will be passed on to our children, our grandchildren, our family, our friends, and you.

Introduction

The year I wrote a book for our sons and grandchildren for Christmas as a part of my Last Will and Testament, my family in Michigan kept asking if the Farm would be in it. Then they'd start regaling me with memories that I should include. Finally I promised them all that the next book would be about the farm, but I warned that they'd all have to be willing to help me.

I made my first "book trip" to Michigan in October of 2000. I had sent my siblings four pages of questions to answer. I spent three or four days with Mother going through photo albums and memorabilia that she had saved. Each day I would ask her questions about a single topic. I found that if I tried to cover more, she became too tired and would say, "Why do you want to know that?" I spent more time getting details from each of my siblings.

In the midst of going through Mother's memorabilia, I found a Diary from 1963. (See Appendix) Although it contains a lot of personal information, there is also data that supports this book about the farm.

While I was there and staying with my sister Darcia, my niece Pamela asked, "Couldn't you somehow add the Granddaughter and Grandson nights that we had on Eleven Mile Road?"

My first response was, "No." I had narrowed the years to include the 50's and 60's, and that nicely covered the major time span of us kids growing up and that of the dairy cows. But her disappointment weighed heavily on me, and I started to think. I had planned to do an Epilogue giving a brief accounting of what the "farm kids" were doing today. So I planned then and there to have an Appendix, even if just for the Grandkids. Of course, I soon found that I'd need it for other material as well.

In the midst of writing and researching this book, Mother, at the age of 78, got her first computer and learned how to do e-mail. This was great for asking the one or two questions that held immediate interest for me. She proclaimed, "This is better than making phone calls." It's just another example of this amazing woman's spirit.

Another trip to Michigan in July 2001 helped me to fill in some gaps of the farm history. I also spent time doing research in Rockford's Historical Museum and the Grand Rapids Public Library. This time in Michigan also led me to some of the "lives" that had touched us on the farm. I believe that their contributions nicely round out this family memoir.

It's been a nostalgic "visit" back to the 50's and 60's for me. During the course of writing this book I've grieved for Dad more than ever before. I know he would appreciate our efforts to recapture the times we had together. I truly gained a new appreciation for my parents and their vision for their lives. I understand the hard work and at times sacrifice that my brothers put into the farm. I saw all of our experiences in a new light. Kierkegaard said, "Life can only be understood backwards, but it must be lived forwards." And so we've continued on with our lives, knowing there's not much that any of us would have changed about our past.

* * *

A special thank you to Evie Opitz and Janet Ratty for proofreading this manuscript.

Table of Contents

Chapter One

Blue Light Memories

On our farm, the color blue taught us more about love than the color red. In addition, it meant Christmas and sharing the memories of Dad and Mom's wedding. All of us could recite the story.

Dad and Mother were married in 1940 in front of a 7-foot Christmas tree with large, blue, electric lights in her parents' farmhouse on Courtland Drive with their immediate families present. Wearing a wine, chiffon velvet dress, which cost her $8, and wine-colored pumps with glass heels, Mother walked down an open stairway as her Aunt Emily DeBoer played the piano. Grandpa DeBoer had told Mother that she couldn't get married until her 18th birthday. Part of this had to do with the fact that Dad was five years older than Mother. (Another detail that we could recite.)

Mother's birthday was December 10. So they waited until the 20th, a whole ten days, for the wedding. Having our parents' wedding anniversary come during the holiday season heightened our sense of celebration. On that day, Dad would start the evening chores (milking) early. He'd come in and take a bath, and without fail they'd go into the big city, Grand Rapids. Also without fail they'd go to the exotic, Chinese restaurant on Division Ave. After that they'd walk downtown looking at the animated Christmas displays in the windows of Wurzburg's or Herpolsheimer's (Herps). We saw all of this as romantic and very Christmassy.

With Mother's birthday falling on the 10th and Phyllis's falling on the 13th, we would search and chop down our tree some time in between those dates, before anyone else in the neighborhood. In the 50's, the trip to the woods would be made with Dad and his hand-sharpened hatchet and axe. The choice of pine trees on our farm was quite sparse; none of them would hold a candle to today's selection. But we always thought that we brought back the best one. (Years later Dar remembers going to Hart's Tree Farm on Young Avenue to pick out a tree.)

We don't remember Mother ever complaining about our choice of trees. She would go about her part of directing us kids in the decorating. The lights were the larger bulbs, and for several years they were all blue. Our ornaments were glass. The final task was hanging the icicles. (1/8 inch x 12-inch strips of aluminum foil.) This job required a lot of patience. They were the prettiest if they were separated from each other and put on one at a time. We would start out with good intentions, then we'd start doing two at a time, then three, and the last handfuls were often just tossed on the tree. But how pretty it'd be with the lights reflecting all that shimmery silver.

The smell of the newly cut pine tree would permeate our house for the next two weeks. Over and over again we'd go into the living room to look at our beautiful tree and enjoy the aroma of the piney scent. To this day, walking past rows of pine trees for sale and inhaling their fragrance brings back memories of Christmas on the farm.

We had a nativity set that would be placed in some honored spot, and Christmas stockings that came out on Christmas Eve. Walking into the living room and smelling the tree before we even saw it, was a child's delight. That was pretty much all the decorating that we did in the country in the 50's. We didn't have any plastic yard-art Santas, pine wreaths on the door, or outside blinking lights.

At this season the barn seemed to be more inviting also. For one thing, the body heat of all the cows made it appealing. Dad would always give the barn cats extra milk and the cows extra molasses or grain in honor of the occasion. Perhaps he was remembering the words to the Christmas Carol, "Away In A Manger."

Some years, Mother would take us kids to downtown Grand Rapids. Then we'd get to see the action displays in the big store windows. We'd have to stand in line until it was our turn to get right up to the front. The mechanisms were simple; we would see a wooden soldier drumming on a drum and another character taking off his hat and putting it back on. If we had enough time, we might even get to stand in line to see Santa. We only remember doing this once. Mother even splurged and bought the black and white photo to commemorate the occasion. The great discussion usually was which store had the better Santa—Herps or Wurzburg's.

Downtown Grand Rapids was like a foreign country to us country kids. We saw lights and displays and people dressed up like we'd never seen before. (People wore their Sunday best clothes when they went to Grand Rapids.) It was also us kids' first time to see a black person. We remember Mother warning us not to stare or point if we saw someone; it wasn't polite. (Of course, Phyllis knew all about that from having polio and people commenting on her limping and/or leg brace.) If it was nighttime, we'd drive through East Grand Rapids where the rich people lived. They even decorated the outside of their houses with lights! We'd ohh and ahh and be thrilled to death. Grand Rapids was the ultimate, holiday destination. Chuck remembers thinking as a child that when he grew up he wasn't going to be a farmer; he was going to live in East Grand Rapids.

If we were real lucky, we'd get enough snow so that the roads were covered with a thick, icy base. And one morning, as we were getting ready for school, we'd be surprised out of our boots by the sound of bells. It'd be Dayton Hammer, with his team of horses and a sleigh filled with clean straw to sit on and blankets to keep us warm, waiting in the road to take us to school. This happened only once or twice, but it filled our minds with storybook memories. We didn't even mind picking the straw off our woolen hats and hand-knitted mittens after our sleigh ride. (Chuck remembers Dayton also giving summertime hay wagon rides with the horses.) Dayton kept his horses long after he transitioned to a tractor.

The closer it got to Christmas the more excited we'd get. Mother kept packages hidden in her closet. And of course, we were admonished that if we didn't behave, all we'd get would be a bag of salt or a lump of coal in our stocking. We were told "real stories" about "real children" getting the dreaded lump of coal as their only present. We became model children for those weeks, gladly volunteering without being told.

Gift exchange was always on Christmas Eve. We'd get Dad things like socks and ties and supposedly his favorite, Chocolate Covered Cherries. He'd carefully open the cellophane wrapping, take off the lid, and pass them around for us all to sample. We thought they were just the best things. For Mother we'd get aprons and Evening in Paris perfume. We'd also get her handkerchiefs, as there was no such thing as Kleenex then. To this day, Mother still carries hankies.

The best Christmas Phyllis remembers is after she and Ron had opened their gifts, and they were told to get ready for bed because it was late. As they walked into the kitchen, there were two sleds! They were overwhelmed, as they thought they'd received all they could expect. Phyllis's sled was longer than Ron's as she was taller. They were the legendary, good ol' Radio Flyers. These fabled, speed machines had bright red, steerable, metal runners and varnished wooden slats to ride on. Morning didn't arrive soon enough.

Darcia's best gift was a big doll that she had seen at Harvard Grocery. She really wanted it. Mother told her that someone else bought it, but she did. She hid it and had it wrapped and under the tree to surprise Dar. Another favorite gift was her Barbie Dream House.

Chuck remembers getting softball and baseball gloves, and Ron remembers one time driving home from church when Mother and Dad were pointing out the hoof prints in the snow. That was quite convincing. That year we had to sit in the car while Dad went up to the attic and put Ron's red 20-inch bicycle by the tree.

After opening our gifts, we'd look hard for the longest stocking (our actual socks) to put out for Santa to fill. Usually we'd end up borrowing from Dad because his were bigger. We never supposed that there really was a Santa Claus, but on Christmas Eve we became believers. Each year we'd also leave a snack for Santa—usually fresh cow's milk and homemade, chocolate chip cookies. And sure enough, the next morning our stockings would be filled and the snack eaten.

At the very toe of each stocking would be an orange that fit with ease thanks to Dad's big feet. Fruit in the wintertime was a rare treat. There would also be lifesavers and gum. Christmas Day we'd go to Grandma and Grandpa DeBoer's house for a big Christmas dinner followed by Dad's favorite pie, mince meat, (before time took the meat out of mince meat pie) and Phyllis's favorite, pineapple pie.

The day after Christmas, we'd remove the ornaments and the blue lights from the Christmas tree, even salvaging the icicles to use another year. We'd put the decorations in a special, round, thin wood, covered container and store it in the attic. But the memories of the season were with us year-round. We'd sometimes envy those who had their tree up until New Year's, but we knew that our way of doing it really was the best!

Maybe that's what makes our farm history worthy of note: we didn't necessarily follow the norm of the day. Dad was not only an innovator in his farming methods, but active in community service as well. Even when it came to being people of faith, we jumped in with both feet. We didn't do anything halfway or half-heartedly.

June 1942

Eleanor DeBoer Is Bride Of D. Porter

The home of Mr. and Mrs. John De Boer of Courtland was the scene of a quiet wedding last Friday evening, December 20th, when their daughter, Eleanor De Boer became the bride of Darcy E. Porter, son of Mr. and Mrs. Charles Erwin Porter of Courtland.

Miss Phyllis Nowlin of East Nelson was bridesmaid and Gaylord De Boer, brother of the bride, was best man.

The wedding march was played by an aunt of the bride, Mrs. Garrett De Boer, of Grand Rapids.

The ceremony was solemnized by the blue and silver lights of a Christmas tree with the bridal party grouped around it. Rev. N. D. Chew of Courtland officiated.

Besides Mrs. N. D. Chew, only the immediate members of the family were present.

The newly married couple are now making their home at the John Haag farm in Courtland where they will be happy to welcome their friends.

**Wedding announcement
Rockford Register
December, 1940**

1973 and Mother still fit into her wedding dress. She wore it for the Mother-Daughter Wedding Dress Style Show. It was the oldest dress there.

8

Note the 16-inch TV

**Dayton Hammer bringing us home from school with his horses
and sleigh, 1951**

...and on earth

PEACE

CHRISTMAS GREETINGS
from all of us...to all of you

Eleanor & Darcy

(1958)

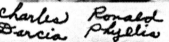

Charles Ronald
Darcia Phyllis

Wurzburg's 1949

Chapter Two

On the Way to Peterson Road

We always thought the story of how Mother (Eleanor) and Dad (Darcy) met was adventuresome and romantic. (It, too, was a story that we could all recite.) A group of young people had been playing ball on a Sunday afternoon and decided to go for a ride to Fisk Nob, the fire tower and the tallest place in the area. Apparently Darcy had been flirting with Eleanor and it continued while they were in the car. Once they reached their destination and started to climb up the tower, Darcy and Eleanor raced to the top and were the first ones up. He kissed her up there and asked her to go see a movie that night. The genesis of the Porter zeal had begun.

Darcy was 23 when he married Eleanor, so he had more years to date. One Saturday night Eleanor was standing on one of the four corners of downtown Rockford by the drug store, and she saw Darcy drive by. She waved, and he waved. However, there was another girl standing on the opposite corner, and she too thought Darcy had waved at her. He drove back around and picked up the other girl. Eleanor wrote him a letter after that incident, and apparently that convinced him that he'd picked up the wrong girl. The rest is history.

During their courtship, Darcy worked the second shift at Federal Mogul and also owned and operated a gas station on the corner of M-57 and US-131. He had a punchboard there that people could pay $.10/punch and see what prize, if any, they won. When it'd get down to the last 1/4 and no one had won the pound box of chocolates, he'd punch the remainder out himself. One day he drove in, and Eleanor was all excited to see that he'd brought her candy, but it was for her mother. Smooth operator, our father.

Darcy spent his childhood as one of seven children living the fulfilling lifestyle of a Kent County farm family. During high school at Rockford, Darcy played football, excelled in chemistry, and won the senior Citizen Award. Because of his good grades, he was in line to receive a scholarship to attend college. But at the last moment, some politics came into play, and the scholarship was given to another. This was a big disappointment in his life.

Eleanor was born and grew up in Rockford. Her father worked at Wolverine doing piecework as a nailer of shoes. She started playing the violin in the sixth grade and played in the high school orchestra. Eleanor followed a business curriculum and graduated from Rockford High School. They purposely kept her diploma to hand out last at graduation because she was the first one to have a job after graduation. Six months later, at the time of her marriage, she received a hand-written letter from Otto Krause, owner of Wolverine Shoe & Tanning Corporation, wishing her happiness in her marriage. (See Appendix)

After their wedding ceremony, they found their car jacked up and in a snow bank, some family member's practical joke. The newlyweds never learned who had been busy. They had to get help to get it out and going.

When Darcy and Eleanor were finally in the car and headed to Grand Rapids, they realized that they had forgotten to pay the preacher, Rev. Nathaniel Chew of Courtland Methodist. So they turned around and took him the $5.00. He then gave them a gift that he'd also "forgotten." After all of that, they decided to go stay in the house that they'd rented ($12/month) on 11 Mile Road.

The following month, Eleanor was surprised and upset when a statement came in the mail for the new suit, hat, and overcoat that Darcy had charged for the wedding. They were also committed to a payment of $12/month towards their furniture—total of $246.58. They stayed in that house only three months—they were frozen out. The snow came in around the windows and right through the wall; there was a drift in their bedroom. Even with a furnace and space heater, they couldn't keep warm. It was with some sadness that they went to live with Eleanor's parents, as they had painted and papered the whole downstairs of the house for one month's rent.

Later that year they bought a house in Rockford on Ogden Street. It was only nine months old, and they paid $2,000 for it. Eleanor's father, John DeBoer, co-signed the note. At this point in time, food rationing, because of the War in Europe, was only a rumor, but Darcy bought 100 pounds of sugar for baking and canning and put it under their bed.

Phyllis Kay was born December 13, 1941 in Grand Rapids, six days after Pearl Harbor was attacked by Japan making America a part of World War II. (She was named for Eleanor's friend, Phyllis Hardy, and Darcy's niece Kay Miller, and was often called PK.) Darcy was so excited that he gave the doctor a foot-long cigar. Eleanor had had her appendix taken out when she was four months pregnant. (That was before the time of ultrasound. The doctor just poised his knife and made an incision—and fortunately, out popped the appendix. Eleanor ended up with only a one-inch incision.) Darcy was rejoicing that there was a live birth—hence the cigar.

Eleanor and baby stayed in the hospital for ten days, and the bill was less than a hundred dollars. But Phyllis Kay's claim to fame was that she had so many living grandparents that there was an article in the newspaper. There were ten! More than one of these grandparents counted all of her fingers and toes when she was born because Darcy and Eleanor were distant cousins. But the only anomaly that we've found is that none of us, except Ron, got our wisdom teeth.

Because of gas rationing, Darcy and Eleanor only lived in their Rockford home for six months. When Phyllis was three weeks old, they moved to Greenville so Darcy could be closer to work. He had been riding a Harley Davidson motorcycle to work. They rented out the Rockford house.

In Greenville, they rented a house at 211 E. Grove St. A couple of months after they moved in, a big, snowstorm came and a neighbor, a retired dentist with Alzheimer's, wandered away from home. His wife came to Eleanor and told her that Mr. Stevensen had run away. So she watched Phyllis, and Eleanor went to look for him. People were all about, including street cleaners that were hauling the snow away.

Eleanor found him on Main Street by the J.C. Penney Store. He had wandered five blocks, barefoot, wearing only his long-legged underwear. She took him by the arm and told him, "Mr. Stevensen, you've got to go back home," and she led him down Main Street. He never as much as got a cold, but being a proper woman, Eleanor was red with embarrassment, walking down Main Street with an old man in his underwear.

They stayed there a year and then moved to Orange Street where they rented until 1944. It was while living there that Phyllis Kay contracted polio when she was 18 months old. They guessed that she might have gotten it from a lake because the family had spent a lot of time at the local lakes that summer.

The first sign Eleanor noticed was that Phyllis Kay walked with a limp. She took her to see their family doctor, Marco Hansen, and he referred them to a specialist in Grand Rapids, but he told her to take her daughter home—she had only bumped her leg! Apparently polio was on the minds of all the mothers, and for any slight problem they were having their children examined.

Time went on, and one day Phyllis fell; her leg could no longer hold her. This time Eleanor took her to a polio specialist at Blodgett Hospital. Darcy and Eleanor carried her around from approximately the age of two to four. She got a leg brace before starting kindergarten at Horton School. One time they stopped at Ramona Park on the way home from the hospital. Phyllis wanted to ride the merry-go-round, but it wasn't open. When the man saw her brace, he started the hand-painted, wooden horses going just for her and gave her the longest ride ever!

This was the time of World War II, and after getting his physical, Darcy received the draft classification of 1A. When he told his employer, Federal Mogul, who made bearings for engines, they got it switched to 2A. This was one of his lifetime disappointments, that of not having the opportunity of serving his country as a member of the armed forces. But during the period of World War II, the Greenville plant was involved in wartime production, and his service there was considered to be most important. Perhaps this was the reason for his untiring and constant government service and community involvement throughout the rest of his life.

Darcy had 100 women working for him. He was given the nickname of "Doc" because he fixed the equipment and kept things going. He started as a set up man and became a foreman. Before he left to farm, he was Assistant Superintendent.

One day, word reached the plant that nylon stockings (These were thigh-high and held up with a garter belt.) were available in town at one of the department stores. There was a one-pair limit. Being a romantic, Darcy stood in line to buy Eleanor a pair, as she didn't have any. Nylons were one of the things that women did without during the War.

In 1944 Darcy and Eleanor decided that what they really wanted to do was to be farmers. Darcy had always said that farming was "in his blood," but he didn't want to be poor like his folks. Eleanor's goal had always been to be a farmer's wife. They bought their first farm on M-57, just west of the Half Way Store (half way between Greenville and US-131). It had 90 acres and they paid $3,700. The barn was on the north side of the road, and the house was on the south side bordering the north shore of Angel Lake.

Many arrowheads were found around that lake; they would even turn up during plowing. The Indians came from Wabasis Lake, four or five miles away, to this hunting ground around the lake. At the northeast side of the lake was a cranberry bog. Darcy and Eleanor would have to get into a rowboat to pick the berries. Relatives would come out from Rockford and Grand Rapids to join in the harvest.

Darcy continued to work at Federal Mogul, as they started out with four or five cows. They farmed with a team of black workhorses, Jack and Jerry. These horses mowed hay, plowed, planted, and pulled wagons. When it worked, a Doodlebug, a "make shift" tractor from car parts, was also put to work.

Rationing was in effect, and Eleanor had to cook on a woodburning, kitchen range. She said, "I couldn't hook up the stove because the farmhouse wasn't wired for a stove. It was wartime, you couldn't get it done. We waited over a year to get an electric water pump. It required a special permit. I had to build a fire in the old range to even make a cup of coffee. The good old days—actually

I enjoyed them. Every so often I get homesick for the range. They were dirty, but nice."

They all took baths in a galvanized tub in front of the stove with the oven door open. It was at this time that George Larsen, an old bachelor, came to live with them and to help on the farm. He had become set in his ways, but Eleanor made him change one of them. She made him take a bath once a week. He was mad; he used to take one only once a year.

Eleanor became a farm wife learning to do things like churning butter, (Grandma Porter gave her a 5-gallon butter churn with a wooden paddle.) canning lard, beef, pork, liver, and even honey. After seeing swarms of bees, Darcy took some of the siding off the side of the house and found it filled with honeycomb.

Eleanor also had a roadside stand where she sold watermelons, sweet corn, and tomatoes from the garden. She bought a fur coat with the proceeds, but when they started going to church, she put an ad in the Grand Rapids Press and sold it because she thought it was too showy.

During this time Phyllis had to lie in bed with her foot in a box so that the sheet wouldn't touch her foot. Apparently this theory went along with not wanting her to put any weight on her foot. She remembers lying flat on her back watching spiral-cut paper placed on a stick on the heat register spin around. George did that to entertain her.

Fordyce Hough stopped by with a church bus, and Darcy carried Phyllis to the bus to attend Sunday school at Oakfield Chapel. He told Eleanor that he felt foolish having someone else taking his daughter to church, and it wasn't long before Darcy and Eleanor started attending too. Rev. Hollis Tiffany was the pastor then.

Eleanor had been leaving spiritual things around for Darcy to read while he waited for his ride (men from Cedar Springs) to work. Evidently it worked, as he wrote in his Bible: "How do I know I am saved? Because I was there! Mother asked me to just believe! I did. Winter of 1947-48." In 1948, under Rev. Hollis Tiffany, a large frame church was given to the members, and they moved it to its present site on the corner of Wabasis Ave. and 14 Mile Road. One Sunday morning when Rev. Tiffany was shaking hands with

Eleanor, he asked if she'd been painting the barn lately because of her red nail polish. She found that amusing.

In the spring, Eleanor was out raking the lawn and putting the leaves in the garden as she burned them. The wind caught the flames and blew the fire east, all the way to Wabasis Road (1 1/2 miles away)—taking a haystack on the way. Swovelands, neighbors to the east, moved the furniture out of their house, believing it was all going to burn. Eleanor made Phyllis stand on the porch while she went out to the road, M-57, to flag down help. Two men stopped, but when they saw the fire, they drove on. Later an official from the county came and did not fine her because she had been denied help by the men.

Another enterprising venture of Eleanor and Evelyn Nicholson was to buy used nylon parachutes from a Michigan Farmer magazine ad. Together they each made a nylon blouse out of the fabric and wore them to church on Easter Sunday.

Mother was in the hospital, on oxygen, with pneumonia three weeks before Ron was born, including New Year's Eve of 1945. She remembers hearing the church bells ring. She did get well enough to return home. Later when she was leaving for the hospital to have Ron, George told her to be sure and bring back a "hired man." Darcy and Eleanor first took Phyllis to Darcy's sister Crystal in Rockford and then drove back to the hospital in Greenville for Ronald Darcy's birth, January 20, 1946. They were happy to welcome a son into the family. Eleanor and baby stayed in the hospital 10 days. Darcy continued his giving of nicknames, and Ron's later became Skip Dip on the Whip.

1946 was also the year that after a wait of 18 months, they got a new car, a 1946 green Dodge. Darcy had said if the car was green, he wouldn't take it, but he changed his mind. They only enjoyed this car for a year because later they traded it for a new Co-Op tractor.

"The decision to quit Federal Mogul and become full-time farmers was a bold step," said Aaron, Dad's brother, "especially after the war and the depression." Federal Mogul worked hard to get him to change his mind, but in 1948, Darcy and Eleanor purchased 120 acres on Peterson Road, between Ramsdell and Myers Lake Road, for $11,000. (Owning a 120-acre farm was especially good as the average farm then was only 80 acres.) After meeting and talking with Mr. Gould, Darcy and Eleanor went into a field west of the house, across from the "sheep barns," and prayed. They decided on a price to offer, and he accepted it.

Payments were set at $30/month. Mr. Gould told them to not make them too high and over extend themselves. He also accepted the contracts from the farm on M-57 as a down payment. (They had divided the farm into parcels and sold them on land contracts.)

The white farmhouse with a tin roof on Peterson Road had sat empty for 12 years. It came with an outhouse, a wood-burning kitchen range, a windmill with a gravity tank above the sink for water supply, a pantry with beautiful glass doors, and two oriental rugs.

Phyllis thought the outhouse was the neatest, fanciest thing because it had five holes: two big holes, one medium-sized hole, and two little holes. The three larger holes were in a row, and the two littlest holes were lower and perpendicular to the other three. She thought this was so the whole family could use it at the same time, but they never did! Outhouses were a part of our lives. Not only did we have one at home, but two at our country school — boys and girls.

These buildings were also of interest to us because later Dad and Mother would recite stories to us of pushing them over on Halloween!! One night, before they were married, three couples, Dad and Mother, Arlene Steinke and her boyfriend, and Althea and John Luyk (sister-in-law Bev's parents) pushed over five! Dad and his guy friends would also put rolls of red, snow fence (made of wooden slats connected by strands of wire) on their cars and let it unroll down the Main Street of Cedar Springs.

It was May when the family moved to the farm that was to be their home for the next thirty-seven years. Only four months later they faced their first, big challenge.

The day they finished planting wheat, Mother had taken Howard, a hired man who had been helping them, back to Grandpa and Grandma DeBoer's where he was staying. Phyllis and Ron were with her as she went to the mill at Porter Hollow to buy buckwheat pancake flour. (She might have spent time looking at the fabric of the feedbags also. She used them to make dresses. Usually a simple A-line dress could be made out of two feedbags. They were all colors with either a small print or flowers.) Dad's grandfather, George Porter, had owned the mill. Even though it had burned two times, he always rebuilt it. The last time he had been 80 years old.

As they returned home and approached the farm, there were cars lined up on both sides of the road like an auction was going on. As they got closer, they could see smoke. Mother stopped the car and left Phyllis & Ron with an unknown lady, later found to be Arlene Cavanaugh, a neighbor who had also just moved to Peterson Street. Mother told her, "That's my house on fire; please take my children."

As Mother drove in the driveway she saw men carrying furniture out. She ran into the house, but the firemen made her leave. They thought that the roof would collapse. Dayton Hammer had used his loader tractor to get the piano out the front door and down the porch steps. (The chipped front steps were a constant reminder and remain to this day.) A passer-by had stopped to tell Dad that the house was on fire. His first reaction had been to throw two pails of milk on the fire as he had been on his way to the milk house. Ralph Pratt and other neighbor men filled milk cans with water and brought them on a trailer to pour on the fire.

The back of the house was all gone. The Fire Department thought the electrical wiring that ran up the wall was the cause. It was an old Delco Lighting System. The chamber pot was left in Phyllis's room—no one had bothered to remove *it*. After the fire was put out, the power was gone. Uncle Aaron remembers helping Dad finish milking the cows by hand.

Dad and Mother spent that night at Dayton and Dorcas Hammer's. (While there, Mother realized that she had lost her wedding ring. The next morning everyone formed a line walking from the house to the barn, and the ring was found!) Ron and Phyllis went to Grandma DeBoer's. Darcy's brothers, Arthur and Aaron, stayed in a car over-night at the farm to make sure the fire was out. The next day Mother's Uncle Gary DeBoer brought them a house trailer.

When Ron returned to the farm the next day, he sat on the steps and said, "My mommy's house burned." Our family of four lived in the trailer for a couple of months. Mother even fed silo fillers (neighbors and hired hands) in the granary in the top of the barn during that time.

We moved into the front of the house while the back was being finished. Dad and Mother declared their first challenge to be a blessing as they ended up with just enough insurance money, $3,000, to modernize the house. We got a bathroom, a new kitchen, running water, and new electrical wiring. The rest of the house was all re-plastered. The ceilings in the dining room and living room were "sculptured" with rounded corners.

It had truly been a year of highs and lows. Before Christmas, Dad and Mother were finally settled in and well on their way to being "real" farmers and a part of their new community. The Porter zeal had been tested, but it was with anticipation that they looked to the next year and a new era for the family on Peterson Road.

Mother in high school

Dad with fox, 1941

First home bought in Rockford for $2,000 in 1941

Farmhouse on M-57
Bought 90-acre farm for $3,700 in 1944

Phyllis in galvanized tub on M-57

Darcy, Eleanor and Phyllis on M-57 farm

**Darcy and Eleanor at
Belle Isle, 1945**

**Easter Sunday 1946
Ron is 3 months old**

Barn on Peterson Road, Co-op E3, 1947

*Mother with
Phyllis & Ron
P.K. with her brace
when our House burned*

Chapter 3

Hard Work and Innovation

Farming, some people say, is the same as gambling. When you plant the seed, you gamble on the price at harvest time. You gamble on whether or not there will be enough sunshine to bring your crop to maturity. You gamble on whether there will be enough rain. You gamble that you'll be able to keep your equipment in good repair, and whether you'll be able to hire the extra hands that will be needed for the harvest.

Basically, it's you against Mother Nature. In the spring we prayed for the snow to dissipate and the fields to dry out enough to plant. The day after we finished planting, we prayed for rain so the seed would germinate. When we applied atrazine to the corn, we did want rain to get it into the soil, and on and on it went.

We wanted rain, and then we didn't want rain—especially if we had a hay crop to bring in. In the fall, the rain would be good for the winter wheat, but interfered with harvesting the corn. And we wanted the corn harvested by Thanksgiving.

The only months that we were free from this weather worry were December through March. Then the cycle would begin all over. It was a topic that consumed us: the weather. Even if there was hay ready to bale and rain predicted for Monday, Dad never worked on Sundays,

On a hot day in June as we brought in the first cutting of hay, Dad would say, "This weather is perfect." None of us agreed, but we didn't say a word. Dad would also say that his father or grandfather used to say, "Dry weather—everyone eats; wet weather—everyone looks for something to eat," and "Dry weather you worry to death; wet weather you starve to death."

On a hot, steamy day in July, he would say, "Today you can hear the corn grow." Grandpa Porter used to say that the corn crop should be knee-high by the Fourth of July and shoulder-high by August. But with the hybrid seed that we used, that saying became out-dated. We wanted our corn to be shoulder-high by the Fourth of July and to have tassels by August.

One year, around 1971, we were facing drought conditions. The crops were on the verge of dying in the fields, and the topic of rain totally consumed us. There's always someone willing to take advantage of a desperate situation, and this was no exception. A man made the rounds of the neighboring farmers with his plan to seed the clouds as they came across Lake Michigan with silver iodide, thereby causing it to rain over our farms. He wanted something like $200 from each farmer. Dad was innovative in his farming methods, and this was one idea that he and the others participated in. It must be that the rain finally did come, as we don't remember a year that we experienced a total crop loss.

Dad was always looking for new and better ways to farm and was often a leader with his practices. As early as 1948-49, we have record of him attending classes sponsored by the Department of Vocational Agriculture. (See Appendix) These classes were held at the old Rockford Public School Building on North Main Street. They were for adult farmers in the area with 15 meetings, once a week from 8 to 10 p.m. in the winter. That year the topic was Dairy Farming; other years the topics were Soils, Crops, Livestock, Farm Management and Income Tax.

Fred Bartlett, who taught agriculture to the day school students at Rockford High School, taught portions of the adult classes. (In the 1960's Mr. Bartlett was the Agriculture teacher and FFA (Future Farmers of America) sponsor for Ron and Chuck at high school.)

Outside speakers, including some from Michigan State College, and Dr. Byram, the local veterinarian, presented some of the topics.

In the 1948-49 course on Dairy, 58 different farmers attended. Other neighbors in attendance were Joe Carlson and Dayton Hammer.

A few years later Dad started putting atrazine on corn so he didn't have to cultivate it so many times. They used to cultivate three times. He also tried disking instead of plowing.

One innovation that Dad put into practice was Strip Crops. This was first done on the 80-acre Holland Farm on 12 Mile Road that he bought. (In the following years, the timber that Dad sold off the farm almost paid for the entire farm.) He planted strips of wheat and corn about 90 feet wide. Not only was it good for the soil to have the crops rotated, but also it was a beautiful sight to see the contrasting colors alternating across the fields. Sometimes hay would be one of the strips. This idea came from the Extension Services of Michigan State and was implemented in 1957 or 58.

Planting on the furrow was a process that ended up being a big time saver, but in the beginning, Dad wasn't too sure how successful it would be. In fact, he used the field beyond the pond, (2nd or 3rd field) west of the road for his experiment. This way it wouldn't show from the road if it didn't look good. He wasn't the only one who watched the progress of this innovation. Often Ralph and Glenn Pratt would stop and go back to look at the field with Dad. The next year, others started using the procedure.

When Dad first started farming, there was a lengthy sequence he followed to prepare the fields. He'd start by disking and then he'd plow the field using a 2-bottom plow. Dragging and then planting and fertilizing followed this. Once the crop was up, he'd cultivate the field to keep the weeds down. This could involve up to five or six steps. Before Chuck and Dar were born, Mother would help him. She would drive the Co-op and Dad used the Farm-All H. They planted about 40 to 50 acres of corn in those first years.

The idea for this new process called "planting on the furrow" came from Michigan State. At first it was only three steps: disk the field, plow the field, and *plant on the furrow.* The idea was that the weeds wouldn't come up as fast, as they had been plowed completely under the furrow. This required major modifications made to the tractor. They narrowed the tractor tires to make them as close to the seat as possible. Reversing them did this. They took the fenders completely off. This process would take 2 1/2 hours.

We must mention that it was a big day when Dad purchased a 3-bottom plow — probably in the late 50's. (When he retired in 1984 he was using a 5-bottom plow and raising about 350 acres of corn.)

The cycle started with planting, and harvesting was the pay off for all of the hard work and innovation. It was also a lot of hard work in the hottest weather. As soon as the planting was done, the first cutting of hay would be ready to cut. In the 50's this was a lengthy process. First, the hay would be cut down using a mower with a six-foot cutter bar pulled by the tractor. Then they used a hay rake; this was a huge spinning disk with 6" tines that put the hay into rows. Then it would have to dry. If it rained or if it was heavy hay, it would have to be raked (rolled over) again. Then the baler would pack the hay into square bales and automatically tie it up with twine. The finished bales would fall onto the ground. A tractor pulling a wagon would come by. With a man on either side of the wagon, the bales would be lifted up to the man on the wagon. (Later the wagon was hooked behind the baler, and a chute sent the bales to the wagon.) This man would be responsible for stacking them tightly on the wagon, so the whole load wouldn't tip off on its way home.

One time Ron and Chuck were taking about 200 bales of hay to sell to a farmer in Ravenna. They only got as far as 13 Mile Road and 1/3 of the load fell over. They restacked it and continued on getting just west of Sparta, and off it fell again. The last time they were close to Ravenna when the bales came off once more. This time Ron and Chuck gave up, called the man, and he came and got the spilled ones. Probably the bales weren't baled tight enough, making them difficult to stack.

Once the wagon of hay got to the barn, someone would have to throw the bales off the wagon to the people working in the haymow. Once again they had to be stacked in the barn just so. One reason was to get as much hay as possible in, and the other reason was so it wouldn't collapse and smother someone, or so people wouldn't fall through the gaps and get stuck. Quite a frightening thought if one was in anyway claustrophobic. (Chuck credits Ron with teaching him how to stack hay in the barn.)

Later, in the 50's, when the barn was getting full of hay, we'd use an elevator to send the bales to the far side or to the upper heights. When the hay got to the beams of the barn, it would be 14-feet high, and some years with good yields it reached the peak, about 30-feet high. (Dad would tease our cousin Louie who didn't like to get too high up in the haymow, because in the Korean War, he became a paratrooper.) When the barn was full, Dad would add extra posts for support under the floor, below in the milking area.

Haying season would also be the beginning of the men tanning to a golden brown. Even Dad would take his shirt off so he wouldn't get a "farmer's" tan. (Brown arms that turned to white where one's shirtsleeves began.) We can remember yet Dad's brown face with the deep wrinkles etched across his forehead, like he was having a continuous good day. When his facial muscles would relax, we'd see the white lines left behind.

In the later years of farming, Dad had a tendency to bale the hay a bit green, which meant it wasn't completely dry, and it was heavy! The extra weight was difficult if a person was handling 1,000 bales of hay on a big day. In addition to who planted corn first, Dad and Dayton Hammer also had an unspoken competition to see who cut hay first.

During hay season in 1963 the first polio vaccine became available. September 21st Mother went to Rockford High School and got enough for all the men and took it to them in the field. The vaccine was injected into a sugar cube; this made it possible for her to transport it. 1963 was also the last year polio was reported in the county; there were eight cases. (In the 1950's there had been a total of 580 cases in Kent County with peaks of 189 cases in '52 and 102 cases in '54.)

In the midst of harvest, it seemed like a perfect day could suddenly become a disaster with a breakdown. The unexpectedness always hung over our heads like a black cloud. Ron and Chuck learned mechanics on site. Even though Dad's plan was to buy one new piece of equipment each year, by the time that the rotation was made, there'd be something operating on its last legs.

At first, Glen Wooster, who had the reputation of being able to fix anything, was our main mechanic. His place was on the corner of M-57 and Ramsdell. Glen repaired tractors and cars alike. His name became so commonplace at our house, and he was so highly regarded by our family that Chuck used to pretend that he was Glen Wooster.

Bill Horton's Oliver dealership in Greenville sold us some of our implements and tractors. Bill was another good mechanic that got us through some tough times. (Phyllis worked in the office in the summers of the early 60's.) Hugh Long on Northland Drive had a Cockshutt/Co-op dealership and then an Oliver dealership, and he became one that we gave a lot of business to also.

Tractors were a farmer's best friends. Some became favorites, and others became notorious. If they weren't capable or always broken down, no work got done. Over the years, Dad had 11 tractors. His favorite was either the 1750 or the 1855. Ron's favorites were the M and the 1750; Chuck's favorites were the 400 and 1855. (In the late 90's Ron tracked down the M in Howard City and restored it. It's still his favorite tractor.)

Dad started farming with a team of horses and a Doodlebug. His first tractor was a Farmall F-12. The progression of tractors that Dad owned follows:

Co-Op bought in 1948—traded in his 1947 Dodge car
Allis Chalmers—traded for the H
Farm-All H—traded on the 560 in Coral
International M—bought on auction—sold to Harpers
Super 55 Oliver with loader—bought in Sparta, traded in Co-Op
560 International—bought in Coral—traded to Bill Horton for 1750 Oliver
400 International—$1200 at auction in March at Carson City
1750 Oliver—bought new from Bill Horton
1855 Oliver—bought new in Rockford from Hugh Long
574 International with loader—bought demonstrator in Benton Harbor area
7045 Allis Chalmers—bought used in Indiana

Filling silo involved some of the earlier harvesting in the summer. Early in the 50's, Dayton Hammer owned the chopper and Carol Patterson owned the blower. (Later Dad owned his own equipment.) The chopper would blow the chopped corn into the silage wagon (a wagon with high sides) that it pulled behind. From there the wagon would be taken from the field to the silo where the silage was then forked off the wagon and onto an elevator with a blower at the end. Those working inside the silo would have the difficult job of leveling the silage as it kept shooting out of the blower. Often this would end up being Ron and Royce Hammer.

All around, silage was difficult, dirty, and smelly. Handling it was one of the least favorite jobs. In the mid 50's, Dad had a new 35-foot silo built, and then there was more work to do. In 1966, he bought a 60-foot by 20-foot silo. With that one he got a silo unloader.

Combining wheat and oats could be dusty, but compared to silo filling, no one complained. There was the added bonus of wheat being a cash crop—products that we sold for money rather than products that we used on the farm. So the larger the yield, the better it was for everyone. Dad had an Allis Chalmers combine. When the grain bin on the combine was full, someone would drive the truck "Big Blue" along side to collect the grain. (Big Blue would hold 200 bushels of wheat and was Dad's first big truck.) Wheat would be transported to Horton's Farm Store in Greenville. In 1960 it sold for about $2.40/bushel, and in 2000 it still sold for about the same price. Interesting. Dad would use his cash crop to pay his spring fertilizer bills.

The last harvest of the season was picking corn. We'd have to wait until there had been at least one hard frost for the corn to harden. This would generally start about October 15. Dad began with a one-row picker. He could do about 4 or 5 acres a day. His first mounted two-row picker he bought with Dayton Hammer. It was a big job to get it mounted onto the tractor. From the picker, the ears of corn would fall into the wagon pulled behind. Then they'd be taken to the farm, shoveled onto the elevator, and dumped into the corncrib.

It wasn't until 1972 that Dad bought a corn dryer. It was noisy and ran day and night for weeks. That first one Dad bought used, and it caught on fire. In 1973, Dad bought a 4-row International

Combine that picked and shelled the corn. This was a change as it meant he kept high moisture corn in one silo.

There was no doubt about it, harvesting involved a lot of hard work, and Ron and Chuck put in more than their share of hours. Dad was always good to reward those who worked for him with small extras. In the 60's he'd have Mother buy cans of pop by the case and keep ice cream bars in the freezer. He'd say to take a break between loads of hay. But then there were the times that he'd push and work until dark in the fields. It was a big day when he started paying hired help a dollar an hour. He knew that he had to be somewhat competitive to keep his workers.

In the 50's, before cans of pop, we'd fill glass, Mason jars with ice cubes and water for the men to take to the field. Sometimes Mother would drive to where Dad was working with a plate of hot food. When Dad started farming on Peterson Road, Mother became a master detective at tracking him down in the fields. He did custom work for three or four years using Uncle Gary DeBoer's Allis Chalmers baler that made small, round bales. At times Mother would have to look for the tracts on the road to see which field he had gone to next.

Once Dad lost his wallet with $60 in it. Mother was upset and went to the field to look for it. She rolled over almost every bale of hay in the field, and it was a hilly field. She found a snake that scared her, but she also found the wallet!

With all the work ethic that planting and harvesting taught us, there is one more gift that we inherited from Dad—being able to take a quick nap. In the midst of the busyness of farming, after the big noon meal, Dad would tell Mother to wake him in so many minutes. The exact time would vary from five to seven to ten to twelve to fifteen minutes. During that time, we didn't make a sound; we didn't even start clearing the table or washing the dishes. Dad would lie on a couch in the summer time or if it was cold out, he and Ron or Chuck would wrap up in Indian blankets, blankets kept special for their naps, and lie on the registers. To this day, all of us kids are able to lie down for ten minutes, fall asleep, and get up refreshed—a wonderful gift we inherited from Dad.

Why Do We Work.?

Thank God every morning when you get up that you have something to do that day which must be done, whether you like it or not. Being forced to work, and forced to do your best, will breed in you temperance and self-control, diligence and strength of will, cheerfulness and content, and a hundred virtues which the idle never know.

Charles Kingsley

This is Dad's handwriting. He had copied this proverb by Charles Kingsley and kept it on his bulletin board over his desk.

Dad and Dayton Hammer, 1951

Dad's Farmall M which Ron later found and restored

Phyllis and Ron with Allis Chalmers and combine

Farm photo, June 1962

First strip farming on "Holland Farm"

Dad with 574 International, 1974

Dad with 403 International self-propelled combine, 1974

Grandson Andy sitting in Grandpa's *red* pickup, 1974

**Dad with Chuck and grandson Andy
1855 Oliver bought new in 1976**

Grandson Tom with 1750

Ron and nephew Fred with 1750

**Dad and Chuck by the last tractor Dad purchased,
7045 Allis Chalmers**

Chapter 4

Heartbeat of the Farm Family

Mother's organizational skills were just as sharp as Dad's. She just put hers to work in a different venue. Her main concerns were feeding and clothing us, keeping the house clean, keeping us up with the news and/or what was current, tracking all of Dad's comings and goings, raising us kids, helping Dad when needed, showing hospitality, being a sounding board for Dad's plans, doing church work, being a good neighbor, feeding and housing hired men, and . . . on and on the list could go. Suffice it to say, she was a strong woman and the heartbeat of our family.

Mother and Dad were a team. Dad was innovative in his farming and herd raising, while Mother was just as industrious, innovative, and dollar-stretching with the activities that directly affected her. The only time that they "went their separate ways" was the election of 1976. Not until later did she tell Dad that she'd voted for Jimmy Carter for President. For the next four years, if something wasn't to Dad's political liking, Mother would be reminded of her wayward voting.

Even on a shoestring Mother kept our farmhouse as fashionable as she could. Once she painted the living room walls navy blue—that made some tongues wag. Or she'd announce at the supper table that gray and pink were the "in" colors this season. Our house was the site of many family bridal and baby showers. We entertained pastors and missionaries. Hired men stayed with us for extended periods of time. Once a family of three stayed in our upstairs for the summer months. They were pipe liners—bringing natural gas from Alaska to the states, we think. All of this, and we had one, small bathroom.

When we moved into the house there was one large (3 foot x 3 foot) heat register in the whole house from the wood/coal-burning furnace. Later others were added that were approximately 18-inches square; that increased the total number of registers to four. The one in the kitchen was the best and warmest. We'd often fight over who got to stand on it. As it was in a corner, there was no sharing. It was also the register that we laid our wet mittens on. Often we would find Dad's pair of work shoes sitting there to warm up before he went out, or we'd tip our own boots upside down to warm them before leaving for school or chores.

The register in the living room was second best when it came to heat production. But it was the best one for entertainment, as we could get warm and watch TV at the same time. We'd stand on it until we were so hot we couldn't stay any longer; after we cooled off and felt cold, we'd return to the register. It would become an on-again-off-again cycle. The least favorite register was in the dining room. It gave forth the least amount of heat, and it was in our least used room, i.e. the lowest social possibilities. The fourth one was in Dad and Mother's bedroom. The upstairs had no registers. It was hot, hot, hot in the summer and just as cold in the winter.

Before the fire, our living room had been a parlor and our dining room had been the living room. (This arrangement was the predecessor to today's living room and family room.) Both rooms had wood floors with oriental rugs. Visiting women would assure Mother that the rugs were indeed authentic, but she'd always say she didn't think so. The living room rug was light gray with dark designs, and the dining room rug was golden brown with bright colors in the design. Mother was always rearranging the furniture. Once she even switched the rugs from one room to the other.

The windmill generated our water before the fire. If the wind wasn't blowing, there was a pump jack with an electric motor. Besides a pipe to the house, there was a pipe to the cow barn. The first year on the farm, the windmill blew over. Dad said, "That's the best thing that ever happened!" and he put in a water pump. (Dad was terrific at seeing the good side of a bad situation, and those of us who are optimists have him to thank.)

Our home was our sanctuary. Around our kitchen table we shared the events of the day, the plans for tomorrow, read the Bible and prayed, and enjoyed some of the best food of any farm family. Mother served meat and potatoes for every noon meal and evening meal, and without fail the food would be passed to Dad and the men first because, "They had been working hard." We all liked Mother's meat loaf and escalloped potatoes. Chuck's favorites were her ham and mashed potatoes, and Dar liked Mother's made-from-scratch macaroni and cheese. Ron's favorite was her baked beans, and Phyllis especially liked her goulash. Meat would always be cooked so you could cut it with a fork or so it fell off the bone. We didn't know about "medium and rare," only "well done." Salad would be lettuce with mayonnaise and bananas. Everyone's favorite was mother's homemade rolls and cinnamon rolls. Our meals always ended with a dessert, and often it was homemade pie; we all loved her huckleberry pie.

Sometimes at the table Mother would share her tales of growing up and the chores she had to do. We'd laugh at her story of her brother saying he had a sunstroke and her being left to work in the garden. She'd also tell tales of how Grandma DeBoer would get Grandpa to "see things her way." If she wanted/needed a new rug in the living room, by using the scissors or a knife, the worn spot would miraculously enlarge. We never talked about anything referring to sex or even said the word out loud, and instead of saying the word "pregnant," Dad would say, "She's P.G." And then there was the "burp box" that sat on the table. In her on-going crusade to give us a proper upbringing, Mother would fine anyone who burped at the table 25¢.

Today we still have memories of Mother getting out the biggest Pyrex mixing bowl, the yellow one, and starting to make the bread dough. Dar says some of the best times she spent with Mother was watching this process. (For the bigger batches she used a bread-maker pail.) She usually used three or four packages of yeast and ended up with four loaves of bread and two cookie sheets of rolls—cinnamon and plain. They smelled so good fresh from the oven. She would spread butter over the tops and then waxed paper followed by dishtowels to keep them soft and warm. By dinnertime we would have sneaked several from the pan and eaten them while they were still warm.

Mother never used recipes. People would ask her for them, and they would always end up being disappointed. Moreover, we daughters never learned to make her bread and pies, and our husbands were disappointed as well. We also have memories of Mother making her own version of pizza when it first hit the scene. She would use cookie sheets for her pans. We'd spread newspapers in the living room and eat on the floor like a picnic. In the 60's, it was pretty much every Saturday, and we watched wrestling at 6 p.m.

All this cooking and baking and wonderful meals produced mountains of dishes and pots and pans to wash. We washed them all by hand, rinsed them, and stacked them in the dish drainer. When it was full, we had to start drying them with a dishtowel and put them away. The towels were thin cotton, and we would use four or five. The sink was white enamel with drain boards on either side. Washing dishes was a two-person job.

Mother also gave her babies their baths in the kitchen sink. Friends would be amazed to see Chuck and then Dar bathed in the kitchen sink. (In 1967 Mother gave her first grandchild, Fred, his first submerged bath in her kitchen sink.) Later she did get a dishwasher but always said she didn't mind washing dishes. Surely a farm kitchen is the best place for a dishwasher.

One thing that we did learn was house cleaning. Mother kept the neatest, cleanest house. She'd sweep the floor of the kitchen, all the way out to the back steps, after each meal. She said the men always "tracked in." Our house was always "picked up" as well. There was an entryway where work jackets, hats, and boots were kept. We remember pushing the vacuum almost every day and dusting once a week. The kitchen floor was scrubbed on hands and knees every other week.

Every spring we did spring house cleaning. Because our furnace burned wood and coal, there was smoke residue that accumulated. We would wash all of the walls in the kitchen, including the ceiling and woodwork. Sometimes we'd go over the walls to get the first coat of dirt off, and then go over them a second time to really get them clean. We would scrub all of the woodwork in the dining room and living room as well, and we'd take all of the curtains down and wash and iron them. This was a BIG job, and one we didn't look forward to.

One chore we did anticipate was opening up the front porch and cleaning it. It was screened, and we lived there most of the summer. It faced north and was shaded by our large maple trees. It was always cool on a hot day. We would eat out there, and often Dad would take his nap there. We kids used the top of the porch steps to get on our horses. We'd lead the horse next to the porch, go up to the steps to the top, and hop on the horse's back.

Twice a month Mother followed a shopping routine. (This coincided with the milk check coming the first and the fifteenth of each month.) At first she bought groceries in Harvard. (This was interesting for us kids, as there was a tavern in Harvard. We'd always count how many cars were parked outside—and during the day at that!) Mother would alternate between shopping at Dow's, which was a larger store and Hough's whose owners attended our church. Later they both attended our church. And much later than that, after the death of their spouses, Mrs. Dow married Mr. Hough: a nice merger of competitors.

In either store, every item on the shelves would have its own price label. As the groceries were taken to the checkout, they'd be hand totaled on an adding machine. This process required that the numbers were punched in and then a handle pulled to register them. For each grocery item the process was repeated. The whole procedure took awhile. We did progress to the large cash registers and a push bar replaced the handle, but the price of each item still had to be entered by hand.

One time when we went to shop at Dow's, they had a large, framed print of the ocean on display. They were having a drawing to give it away. Mother wrote her name and put it in the box. A few weeks later when we were there again, Mr. Dow asked Mother if she liked that picture, and of course, she said, "Yes." He said, "Well, that's good, because it's yours!" She could hardly believe that she had won something. The picture came home with us and was immediately hung in the living room.

Mother also shopped at Guilfoyles near Ziegenfuss Lake. That store had to be the forerunner to Wal-Mart. It was a hardware store/

grocery store/tackle and bait/small parts store. They too were friendly. Later she shopped at the Rockford Kroger store where Chuck would get to pick out cereal with the baseball cards he wanted, and starting in 1959 she would often venture even further away to Meijer Thrifty Acres in Plainfield. Mother had a budget and out of it she not only bought groceries, but clothes and gifts. Two things she didn't have to buy were milk and beef.

We drank milk with all of our meals. Mother kept it in various sized glass jars in our refrigerator. The tops of all the jars would be thick with the cream that would rise to the top. None of us liked the thick taste of cream. We'd always stick a knife into the bottle and "stir up the milk" before pouring it. We drank "raw" milk—it wasn't pasteurized. City folks thought that was unhealthy and unwise, and we thought that "city" milk tasted horrid and refused to drink it. Neighbors were shocked to hear that as babies Mother fed Chuck and Dar "raw" milk mixed with Karo syrup. She'd bring the milk to a boil, add the syrup, and that was their formula.

We not only ate well, but a lot. When Phyllis and Ron (Dolislager) were dating and he stayed for a meal, he said it was the first time that he had a whole steak to himself. A roommate of Phyllis's from Taylor University said it was the first time she ever sat at a table for dinner and there were more potatoes in the serving bowl than people around the table. We had so much beef to eat that bologna and hot dogs were wonderful treats for us.

Sweet corn season was a highlight for our entire family. Dad would plant several rows along the roadside of his field corn. Whoever was available would pick the corn, and then we'd husk it and boil it. After buttering it and adding salt, we could eat our way through two-dozen ears. We'd pile the corncobs in front of our plate and proudly count them. Our hired men all joined in the good-natured banter/competition at our kitchen table. But the all-time family record was 8 or 9 ears held by Mother.

During the harvesting season, Mother also had the responsibility of feeding the men who came to help. This could mean eight to ten extras when it was the bean threshers. She would feed them meat, potatoes, baked beans, homemade rolls, and a variety of pies. The wives would always ask their husbands what they'd been fed at these times, so the pressure was on to be as good or better than the last place they had eaten.

We usually started our days with Wheaties or Shredded Wheat and toast. The thought of toasted homemade bread with butter still makes our mouths water. That first bite of crunchy bread and salty butter was wonderful. Dad was the best toast butterer; he'd spread it to the very edges for us. He'd also cut our toast into four pieces. On Saturdays, Mother would make pancakes for lunch, another of Dar's favorites. One year, telling Mother that he wanted us kids to know how maple syrup was made, Dad tapped our beautiful row of Maple trees by pounding in a small piece of pipe and hanging a pail to catch the sap. Mother made the syrup on the stovetop. It took so many hours of boiling that they only did it once. (It took 20 gallons of sap to make one gallon of syrup.)

Later Dad fought to save those same Maple trees that lined our property. As the county was preparing to improve the road with black top, they were going to take down 15 to 20 trees. This made Dad mad, and he went out and really yelled at them. We often joked that he said, "Over my dead body," but then maybe he did, because they changed their minds about cutting most of his trees, and took only four or five.

Sunday evenings we remember having crackers and milk or bread and milk. We'd sprinkle salt on the bread to make it taste better. Sometimes we'd have soup. Mother always added milk and butter to the soup, not water. No wonder it tasted so good! If we had company over after church, which was often, we'd have sloppy joes, chips, pickles, and either pie or brownies. If we had cookies, they'd be chocolate chip or peanut butter. The later would be the ones with the fork marks pressed onto the tops.

Neighbors made a conscious effort to look after one another in the 50's. The ladies would always be attuned to a death in the neighborhood. They would take food to the grieving family. This would usually be a complete meal including rolls and dessert. Other times that they'd take food might be for an extended illness, injury, or the birth of a new baby. It showed their caring and concern. Also in the 50's, we were aware of cars that passed our farm on the gravel road. A wave of the hand was appropriate for us, and the passing neighbor would give us a toot on the horn. Neighborly rituals seem to have passed away with the demise of the farm family.

During the winter months, we kids would make many trips to the basement to bring up canned goods. There were shelves filled with the bounty of Mother's labor from the summer and fall months. Mother would usually can 100 quarts each of tomatoes and beef, (We've never found hot beef sandwiches as good as her's anywhere!) 80 quarts each of peaches and dill pickles, 40 quarts each of green beans and corn, 20 quarts of pears, and several pints of jam. At times we kept carrots stored in dirt in the basement as well. (We called it the basement, but it was actually a Michigan cellar. Cement blocks supported a few of the walls and portions of the floor had concrete, but there was a lot of sod exposed. It was a dark, damp place.)

Most of the vegetables for the canning came from our garden. We'd grow green beans, cucumbers, dill, tomatoes, radishes, carrots, peppers and onions. Later we grew pumpkins. We also had a strawberry patch. We kids learned lessons about diligence from picking paper grocery bags full of green beans and then snapping them. Because the garden was close to the road, east of the house, Mother always wanted it to look good. This meant constant weeding for her and us kids.

Typical of every farmer's wife of those times, every Monday Mother would take the dirty clothes down to the basement. She'd fill the Maytag washer with hot water and set the galvanized tub on the rinse rack. Fels Naptha was the commonly used soap. The white clothes would be washed first proceeding down to the dirtiest work clothes, all the time using the same wash water. After the load was done, she'd put the clothes through the wringer, and they'd fall into the rinse tub filled with cold water. After thoroughly plunging them up and down by hand in the water, they'd be put through the wringer again into the laundry basket, and the process would start over with the next load being put into the washer.

Once Mother caught her lower arm in the ringer. Fortunately she was able to hit the release lever and free her arm. Because of this danger, she seldom let us kids put laundry though the wringer, even though it looked like a fun job. There were tricks of the trade to making the wringer work without damaging your clothes. Shirts/blouses would be folded with the buttons inside so the wringer wouldn't pop them off. Jeans would be folded in half and you'd start with the legs first. Towels would go one by one, but we'd try to tack on another towel at the very end to keep the flow going through the wringer to lessen the chance of jamming.

If it was summertime, Mother would proceed outside to hang the clothes on the line. She would hang two pieces side to side with one pin. Then pick up the other end and join another piece to it. This way conserved clothespins. Jeans were hung by their waist. Shirts were hung upside down by their side seams. T-shirts were hung right side up by their shoulders. Towels were hung end to end. Sheets were folded in half and hung by their edges, allowing them to fill with wind and billow out. Once the load was hung, we'd get the clothes pole and prop the line up with it. (The year that we had baby pigs is memorable because they'd be under foot while we were trying to hang laundry.)

Periodically we'd go outside and check to see if the clothes were dry. If they were, we'd put them into the laundry basket. Sometimes we'd move the pins slightly so the wet spots could dry as well. The clothespins were wooden, made from one piece of wood, with the top one solid piece and the bottom shaped into two parts. We'd use the separated parts to put on either side of the clothesline to hold the clothes in place. If we'd forced them or if the clothes plus the clothesline was too bulky, they would split and break. It seemed like we were always looking for extra clothespins. Seeing the line filled with laundry, on a sunny day, gently blowing in the breeze was a beautiful sight to a farmwife and provided a nice, clean smell to our clothes.

In the winter, more creativity was called for. Clothes would be hung in the attic where Mother had clothes line strung, or they would be laid over clothes racks set on the registers. Mother always preferred hanging them outside, but sometimes she would find out it really wasn't warm enough, and her clothes would be frozen stiff as a board on the line.

This laundry routine lasted until 1959 when Dad ordered a new automatic washer and a dryer. They were installed upstairs—just outside the bathroom. However, Mother was so leery of the new machines that she refused to let him trade in her old Maytag. She kept it in the basement just in case the new one didn't get her clothes clean enough. (Phyllis remembers this vividly. Going to Taylor

University that fall, she was under the impression that the added expense would make her family undergo some hardships. She felt an enormous relief the first time she returned home and saw the new washer and dryer, for surely this meant her education wasn't going to send the family to the poor house.)

Since Monday was washday, then Tuesday was the day to iron. The step in between we called "sprinkling." Everything would be laid piece by piece on the kitchen table. We'd have a bowl of water into which we would dip our hand. Then we'd shake it so the drops would fall somewhat evenly over the entire piece. We'd fold the piece and roll it up. Mother would have a basket full of rolled up clothes to iron.

She purchased a Mangle ironer that she put in the kitchen. She would put the clothes through the opening, like putting them through the wringer, but one end was open. She sat on a chair and operated the roller with her knee. We kids never helped with the ironing as Mother thought it was too dangerous for us. She did get burned once on it. This also explains why Phyllis and Dar were never taught how to iron until they left for college.

Our telephone was a black cradle phone with a rotary dial, and our phone number was VO6-87__. The VO was for volunteer. It sat on the desk in the dining room. Eight families were on one line, but we'd only hear the rings for "our side." Ingrahams' ring was one long and one short; ours was two long; Hammers' was three long, and Pratts' was four long. The phone was to use for business, emergencies, and mostly adults. Kids weren't allowed to talk very often. If you wanted to use the phone and someone else was on, it could be frustrating. Some neighbors talked on and on it seemed. If there really was an emergency, we'd break in and ask if we could please use the telephone. Other times we'd just pick up the receiver and "listen in." You could tell by the clicks if someone did that while you were talking.

Another interesting fact about the farmhouse was the noises that it'd make. Walking from one room to another would make enough creaks and groans to let everyone know you were coming. But the most difficult to navigate quietly was the stairway. Getting up the stairway without making a sound was nearly impossible. The contracting and expanding of the house caused by the weather could keep a person awake at night. But the scariest sound was of something scurrying up and down the insides of the walls. We discovered that we had red squirrels living in our attic, and at times they'd chase each other around and up and down the inside walls of the house. We'd have to alert overnight guests, as the sound would set one's hair on end if you hadn't been forewarned.

Our attic was a large room that never had been finished. It had a proper sized window, an overhead light, and sloping sidewalls, like the upstairs bedrooms. We walked into it through a regular sized door. The floorboards were missing in one corner, and we had to be careful where we put our feet. When Mother emptied the canning jars, they'd be carried to the attic. When we were tired of a toy, it'd go to the attic. We actually had a play space up there for a while. There was a big round-top trunk that we enjoyed looking into also.

Every other year or so, when the attic seemed to have accumulated too much useless clutter, Dad would back the pick-up under the window, and we'd throw "stuff" down to be hauled to the dump. We kids would get into this project and have a ball tossing things and trying to land them in the bed of the truck. Meanwhile Mother would find out what we were tossing, and she'd proceed to "save" some things. This was always a time that Mother would cry because "memories" were being tossed away.

Seeing a movie portraying the 50's is pretty much like looking at our kitchen—complete with mother wearing a housedress covered by an apron. Mother routinely wore dresses until the 1970's when slacks became more commonplace. We had a gray-marbled chrome dining set. An oilcloth always covered it. 12-inch black and white asphalt tiles were laid on the floor, and the counters were covered with black marbleized tile. The sink was white enamel with matching drain boards on each side. We'd put the washed dishes in the dish rack on the left side and pile the pots and pans to dry on the right side.

Dad had a large desk against the south wall of our kitchen. (Johnnie Creek made it.) We all thought this was a wonderful thing—Dad had a place to keep and do his bookwork. But when it was bill-paying time, he would move to the kitchen table. Phyllis remembers him teaching her how to write checks and helping him with this job. She and Dar both recall him teaching them how to fill out their own federal tax forms.

Mother, however, will always be remembered as the one who had the courage to collect debts for Dad. Usually he waited until the debt was long overdue, then he'd say to Mother, "I'll give you $10 if you'll call up so and so and get him to send the $100 that he owes for custom work last fall." This could involve hay, meat, cattle, whatever. Mother always took him up, and she always got her check!

Above the desk was a large bulletin board. After Chuck and Dar were born, the frame became the marking place for everyone's height. Regularly on birthdays we'd go to the bulletin board and "get measured." Chuck and Dar would stand on the desk; Phyllis and Ron would stand beside the desk. When the desk was moved into the small bedroom, which became Dad's office, the freezer replaced it. This measuring routine continued on with the grandchildren.

Once a month Mother would attend County Home Extension Meetings. The neighborhood ladies would take turns having them in their homes and being hostess. They covered topics that were helpful to life in the country. County Extension agents taught them or the ladies would take turns. (In the 50's these were the ladies that handed out the best, homemade treats at Halloween such as brownies, popcorn balls, cookies and fudge. Later in the 60's, Hammers was the best place to "hit" as Dayton handed out dime candy bars!)

Five years after we moved to Peterson Road, Chuck was born, October 1, 1952. (Mother fed silo fillers the same week.) Chuck was the 5th baby born in the new Greenville Hospital. He was born during a thunderstorm. The lights went out and the nurses held flashlights for the delivery. Grandma Porter came and stayed with us. Mother remained in the hospital five days and took Chuck to church the next day. Fordyce Hough had Dad carry him up front as the newest member of the Sunday school. Chuck was named after both grandpas: Charles for Dad's father and John for Mother's father. (Grandpa Porter died four months before Chuck's birth, but he had been told if the baby were a boy he'd be named Charles for him.)

Unlike today, women only announced their pregnancy when they absolutely couldn't fit into any of their clothes. Mother would wait until she was five or six months along before she'd tell anyone. We all had memories of Mother lying on the couch wearing her red-orange duster while she was pregnant with Chuck. She kept us busy bringing her glasses of soda water for her heartburn. Only a few months later, it seemed, she was back on the couch again, this time expecting Darcia. She was in the hospital two days before Dar was born on January 7, 1954. The doctor told Dad he had time to go home and milk the cows. As Dad returned, Mother was being pushed into delivery. Then he wished that he'd never left. When Mother came out, it was time for visiting hours. She stayed in the hospital five days, and once again Grandma Porter came to stay with us. Darcia was named after Dad, and she was given Mother's middle name, June.

Dad declared that he had a "Rich Man's Family," two boys and two girls. He'd often refer to Chuck and Dar as his second family, and Mother called them her twins as they were only 15 months apart. Chuck would steal Dar's bottle out of the diaper bag in church and at home. This earned him the nickname of "Jughead." Later, Mother made us stop, as she was afraid it would stick for the rest of his life. Dad nicknamed Darcia, "Honey Dar," and that name did stick.

The bedrooms of the farmhouse were now full, and the extra hands all contributed to making farming on Peterson Road a rewarding life with the farmhouse the center of much activity. Mother surely did fulfill her dream of wanting to be a farm wife. And in the process, she became the heartbeat of our lives.

1952

**Mother with neighbor
friend, Dorcas Hammer**

**Farmhouse on Peterson Road. Note grassy driveway. House
had set empty for 14 years. Mother, Phyllis, Ron.**

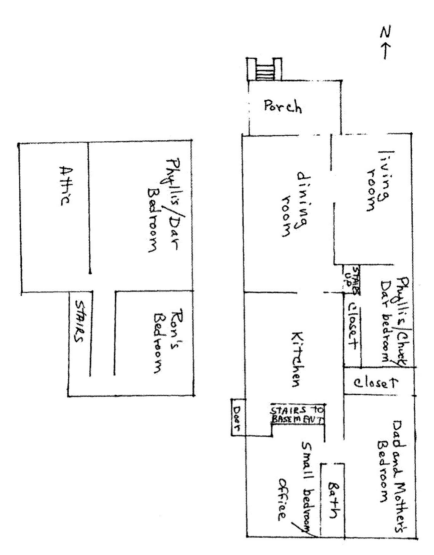

Floor plan of the farmhouse.

**Jealous Lassie watching the cats eat.
Note 50's floor of black
and white tiles.**

**1952. Dar's first birthday with big
brother helping. Note Mother with
her full apron.**

Our 2nd family – Dec. '54

Dad measuring Dar on her birthday.

Mother and her boys, Ron and Chuck, 1955

**Mother's Day breakfast served in bed by Chuck, Dar
and Lassie.**

Trust in the Lord with all thine heart; and lean not unto thine own understanding. In all thy ways acknowledge Him; and He shall direct thy paths.

Proverbs 3:5+6

This is Mother's handwriting. She would write this Scripture in every Bible that she gave to kids and grandkids.

67

**1950, 10th wedding anniversary
gift from relatives.**

**Jackie, our border collie, named after
Jackie Onassis.**

Chapter 5

Country School and Beyond

It was a sure sign of spring when we started riding bikes to school again. The roads were gravel and sometimes soft and sometimes bumpy with ruts. They didn't get paved until Dar's last year at Courtland Center. We had to be skillful and careful. Our bikes didn't have gears, and their balloon tires had no special treads. All of our bikes did have metal baskets. We carried our lunches and anything else we wanted at school in them. More than one glass-lined thermos was broken as the bike rider crashed on the way to or from school.

Riding our bikes was a kind of social event for us. We'd usually ride with someone. Phyllis would stop and get Ann Pratt. Ron would ride as far as Pratt's or Ingraham's with her and continue on with someone else. Dar would ride in the morning with Chuck, who rode with Brian Ingraham, but was always left behind because of being slower and having a smaller bike that didn't go as fast. Royce Hammer was one of the fastest bike riders; it was hard work to keep up with him. The Cavanaughs usually walked, while the Ingrahams seemed to ride their bikes whenever the weather permitted, and they did this as very young children.

Being strong enough or big enough to start riding your bike to school was a great day. Darcia flew to the head of the line as Mother let her ride when she was in kindergarten. A five-year-old riding 2 1/2 miles one way was noteworthy. Dar does admit to being scared going home alone on her bike. She did this not only as a kindergartener but in first and second grade also because they were let out early. Returning home she remembers first watching for Gordon Pratt's farm and then being really happy to make it to the corner of Petersen and Young. Getting to Cavanaughs and Pratts was even better because she then had to only get up the big hill to our farm (We'd usually end up walking our bikes up the hill.), and the rest of the way home was in the shade of our big maple trees.

Riding our bikes was wonderful freedom as well as a means of being self-sufficient. We also learned to look out for the younger ones, as we would have to slow our pace for some of them until they caught up with us. Our bikes were the biggest and best things we possessed. They were probably the only status symbol in our lives. And getting a new bike was a BIG event.

Wheaties had miniature license plates in its boxes for a while. We put them on our bikes and thought we were really cool. It didn't take much to make us happy. We also traded them to get the one we wanted. Phyllis had to ride Mother's old bike. It had been repainted, by hand, a medium blue. This meant no stripes or logo. The frame was narrower than the newer bikes. (The space between the handle-bars and seat was about 12 inches.) Making a quick stop usually meant falling against the front bar and hurting yourself. We did a lot of trading bikes for the ride home—and only the kind-hearted would trade with Phyllis for her old bike. Her last year of country school, eighth grade, she finally got a new bike.

When the roads were muddy or the weather was bad, our parents would have a car pool. Usually the Hammers, Pratts and our parents would alternate weeks. We never would have passed any safety tests. Of course, we hadn't heard of seatbelts then, but as we sat two and sometimes three deep all across the back seat we couldn't have used seatbelts anyways. One day when we were walking, Fred Carlson, Ann's uncle, stopped and offered us a ride home from school. Phyllis didn't remember him and wouldn't accept his offer of a ride. Apparently she had been told not to accept rides with strangers even in the 50s.

Walking home, we'd linger and play along the way. We had short cuts too. There was one from Peterson to Young, cutting off the corner, and one from Young to 13 Mile Road. The small paths were hard to find and sometimes we'd sort of get lost. Then if Mother came to get us and we weren't on the road because we were in a field taking a short cut, we'd be in trouble. So if we took a short cut, we'd have to walk quickly so we'd be in view of a possible ride home.

Of course, we'd stop to play and sometimes to gather things along the way. Pussy willows were a big find. They would be in the swamps on 13 Mile Road and also on Peterson Road west of Cavanaughs. We'd pick up acorns in the fall and hickory nuts, but leave the messy walnuts alone. Sometimes we'd fight. Once Ann Pratt swung her dinner pail at Bud Feikema and knocked a permanent tooth loose because he had been picking on her. We would always "wait" for a phone call from parents after incidents like this.

During the summer or on Saturdays, Chuck and Dar would stop and play in the creek with Brian and Helen Ingraham. Other times, Dar would go down the hill the other way, east, to play with Diane Hammer.

School started at 9 a.m. This meant that we had to leave home by 8:15 a.m. As we approached school, we would see the plain building and a wood shed. To the east was a small ball field and south of that was a swing set and teeter-totter. Immediately behind the school were two outhouses—one for the boys and one for the girls, and to the west of the school along the edge of the road was a 20-foot wide swale where we'd play house and make forts.

After leaning our bikes against the schoolhouse (We didn't get bike racks until the 60's.) we'd go in the east door and up four steps to the cloakroom. There we'd hang our jackets, leave our boots and lunch boxes. Then we'd go into the schoolroom. When Phyllis started Courtland Center in second grade, all eight grades and kindergarten met in one room. There were black boards on the west wall and north wall. Depending on the current teacher's preference, his/her desk would be at the west or south. Our desks were almost always in rows facing the west. They were desks and seats in one piece. The top lifted up and the "belly" held all our books. We'd often lift up our desktops so we could talk to a neighbor and not be seen. Some students would keep "treats" in their desks and snack during the day.

School would start after Labor Day and end at Memorial Day. In the early 50's, we'd get a week off to pick potatoes. The school day began at 9 a.m. with the Pledge of Allegiance. The teacher would go outside and ring a hand bell to bring us in. On special occasions, she'd let one of us ring the bell. We'd have a 15-minute recess at 10:30 a.m. and an hour lunch at 12 noon. (Kindergarteners left at 11:30.) In the afternoon there would be another recess at 2:30 p.m.; this would be the time that first and second graders would leave for home. The rest of the students stayed until 4 p.m.. The last 15 minutes of the day, we'd straighten up, wash the boards, and take the papers out to burn. Then the process of biking, walking, or carpooling would be played out in reverse.

In 1953 or '54 another room was added to the school and another teacher was hired. Kindergarten through 3rd grade moved into the new room. This addition not only brought us a smaller student/ teacher ratio but indoor plumbing! It was difficult to say which we appreciated more. And yes, these were the times that we were instructed to hold up one finger or two fingers depending on why we were asking permission to use the restroom. Supposedly this was so the teacher could gauge how long we might be gone. The teachers were also our janitors. At times they would hire some of the boys to sweep the floor and bring in the wood or coal. Herm Feikema worked for Mrs. Thompson for $5 a month. He later hired Ron Clement to help him for $1 a month.

Depending on the teacher, we would have rigorous instruction and get through our books in a year's time, or we would listen to sermons and watch chalk talks. When the later happened one year, the mothers started making surprise visits to school to observe the teacher. (Dad was on the school board.) Evidently we did cover enough of the basic subjects because when we got to Rockford High School, we could hold our heads high and make the honor roll with little difficulty. Science would be the one field where we were sorely lacking.

Our class size was always small. Phyllis had a class of four, and Ron had a class of four. In Chuck's last class at Courtland Center there were five, and Darcia's last class of 2nd grade had five or six. Sitting in a classroom with four grades and listening, even subconsciously, to all the various lessons gave us a constant review of our basics and a preview of what was to come. This was in addition to our own studies. Reading, *Jim and Judy* and then *Dick and Jane*, spelling, arithmetic and penmanship were emphasized. The older kids would help the younger ones. Sometimes we'd go into the lower classroom to assist the teacher there.

Buying books was an interesting process. We'd go to Skinner's Drug Store in Cedar Springs. There would be huge piles of used books in varying condition and prices, and there would be some new ones. Mother always bought Phyllis new books as an incentive to get good grades. Ron got used books as did Chuck and Dar if they were available. Every year more than one kid would end up with books that had all the answers written in. This was a frustration for the teacher as it was usually the poorer students. She'd caution, "You can't be sure that those answers are correct; you'd better work those problems yourself and find out."

One time a teacher decided that we should be taught square dancing. This was something that the whole room could do together. She called it "rhythm games." We kids were all for this, and we practiced a few times. It didn't take long for the "rhythm games" to be "exposed," and parents were calling each other saying, "Do you know that your kids are being taught to *dance* at school?" Needless to say, our dancing careers were short-lived.

We received report cards every six weeks. At the end of the year almost everyone would pass, but not always. Sometimes extra smart kids would be offered a chance to skip a grade. Phyllis was promoted from kindergarten to second grade when she attended Horton School. Mother had taught her so much when she was laid up with polio that kindergarten held no challenge for her. Ron skipped 4th grade because he was bored and had nothing to do. Darcia's teacher was going to have her skip third grade, but that was the year she was moving to Lake's Elementary, and Mother didn't think it was a good time to do it. Phyllis and Ron finished eighth grade at Courtland Center. Chuck went to Lake's for 5th and 6th grades.

Lunchtime we put our desks in small groups and opened our metal lunch boxes. Some were blue with rounded tops to hold the thermos and others were square with metal clips to hold a thermos. We ate whatever Mother had packed, but trading was always an option if another person was willing. Phyllis remembers dill pickle sandwiches; Ann Pratt remembers pickled tongue. If the weather was nice, we'd take our lunches outdoors. One year, we organized a whole Thanksgiving dinner assigning kids what they should contribute to the menu. We enjoyed a rather impressive meal.

After lunch we'd play house or play fort. We named the swale by the school Bunker Hill. We made rooms up there using sticks to mark the walls, leaving openings for the doors. By the time we'd be done "making" the house or fort, the bell would usually ring. Sometimes we'd all play work-up. This was softball where everyone would take a position and there'd be three batters. As one struck out, we'd all move up or around a position. Then we'd start again at recess where we'd left off at lunchtime. When we had teachers who "didn't have much to teach us," our lunch hours would stretch out a long time. On some Friday afternoons we'd have a ballgame with another school. Capture the Flag was another game we enjoyed. Chuck chipped his two front teeth playing it as he was pushed and fell onto the bike rack.

A highlight for us was the arrival of the Bookmobile. Once a month it would come and stay about an hour and a half. All of us would have a chance to go and check out a book until next month when the bookmobile returned. Phyllis often got Laura Ingalls Wilder's books of *The Little House on the Prairie* series. We also would have one or two field trips a year. We'd go to the Grand Rapids Museum. The favorite thing there was to see the mummy whose toes had rotted off. The Shrine Circus was a big event. The mothers would take us. Darcia loved the trapeze artists. The upper grades would sometimes go to the Detroit Tiger ballgames in Detroit. We also had area-wide Field Days in Cedar Springs. This let us compete against other students in physical activities.

The County Superintendent of Schools, Lynn Clark, would visit us once a year and look at the teacher's grade book and attendance book. Apparently that was all the validation that we needed. However, in the 60's a visiting teacher from the County came once a month to see if the teachers had any problems or concerns. She would check on our resource materials, most of which consisted of various filmstrips and a filmstrip projector. We did have penmanship charts across the top of the black board and a map stand with "ancient" maps. Later we got wall maps.

All of us could find our state of Michigan on the U.S. map. We Michiganders carry our state's map on our right hand; to this day we'll proudly point and show anyone exactly where we live. Ronald Jager in *Eighty Acres* has this explanation for the state's unique mitten-shape, "The lakes today shape the Michigan profile as they do because eons and eons earlier, when God formed the world, He rested His hand gently here...."

Teachers did not need a four-year college degree. They could start with just a certificate from County Normal. This was a nine-month program in Cheboygan that was intense in reading, language arts, math and science the first semester and practice teaching the second semester. Teachers went back to school each summer to renew their certificate. When Sue Van Liew came to teach at Courtland Center, she'd had two years experience at another country school. The fall of 1958, her third year of teaching, she earned $3,800. In her first years of teaching, teachers had to pay their own Social Security tax. Sue was at Courtland Center three years. (Thanks to Mother's introduction, she married our milk tester.)

Sue Van Liew Rosenberger says, "Courtland Center was quite an up and coming school in its day. The Board members were education oriented. They also kept good books. The school I taught at before didn't get their reports into the County on time, and I would get paid late. They also provided a music teacher once a week. I had 17 students in grades four through eight the year I came, and the numbers stayed about the same the other years. My second year at Courtland Center the furnace blew up and school was closed for a week for cleaning. Another time the piano tuner found baby mice in the piano. The parents were interested and community minded and helpful. It was a good experience."

Fundraisers were active even then. Each kid would be given a box about 4 inches x 4 inches square filled with seed packets. The whole box was $1.00 and each package was 10¢. Our parents would make the big decision of what to buy, but they never bought the whole box.

We anticipated Christmastime and the school Christmas Program. Everyone would say a piece, and we'd all sing and take part in little plays. The highlight would be Santa bringing small gifts. This would usually be a man in the community. We remember Dayton Hammer and Al Ingraham as especially good Santas.

When Courtland Center was closed in 1963, most of the students went to Cedar Springs High School. The building was sold to Cedar Springs, but later Jim Himes bought it back for $2,000 for the township. Which school you went to depended on the location of your property. Believing that Rockford was the better high school because they both graduated from there, our parents had their farm transferred into the Rockford School District. This meant that they had to pay 5 to 6% more in property tax. Because we transferred, the Ingrahams were also able to transfer as their property was diagonal from ours. (The points touched.) Pratts and Hammers went to Cedar Springs.

By today's standards, Courtland Center wouldn't win any awards, but no one told us that our education might be deficient. A number of students went on to college, others have their own businesses, and some are still in the community as successful farmers. Chuck was Township Supervisor for four years.

Phyllis left her bike behind and got on the big, yellow school bus for the first time in 1955. Immediately she found a seat by Ann Pratt, and together they started their adventure in high school. The friendship that started in second grade continued right on. They met many challenges together starting with working the combination locks for their lockers, to changing classes every hour and having six different teachers and homework, and ending with being co-editors of their senior yearbook. They discovered that they weren't behind in their academics because of country school, but could easily make the honor roll every marking period. Ann went on to become the Salutatorian and Phyllis was also in the top ten of their class of 100. The Porter family tradition of receiving a Bulova watch for graduation began with Phyllis.

The fall of 1959 brought the family a lot of beginnings. Phyllis started college at Taylor University. Ron started high school the same fall, and Darcia started kindergarten. When Dad and Mother drove

Phyllis to Upland, Indiana for the fall semester, it was her first time to see the campus. They unpacked her things and returned home. Mother said she cried all the way back to the Michigan border. She also wrote a letter to Phyllis every day! The family experienced new dynamics at various levels that fall. Once change takes place, there's no going back, except in our memories. Beatrix Potter said it best, "Thoughts of that peaceful part of childhood come like soft music and a blissful vision."

Ron was active in Future Farmers of America (FFA) at Rockford High School. The advisor, Fred Bartlett, kept a scrapbook and reminded us of the following: In 1960, Ron gave the invocation at the FFA Banquet, was a member of the Parliamentary Procedure team that won the District Contest, and participated in the Slave Auction (14 years old @ 135 lbs.). Later Ron was a member of the Demonstration Team: the topic was "Ear Corn Storage;" he received a score of 98 out of 100 on the Dekalb Corn Contest. Ron won the Gold Award on Activities Point Contest and first place in the plowing contest with the "M." Dad coached him by saying, "Don't rush it; take your time." Ron also won the Star Greenhand Award as a freshman.

In 1967, Chuck was chairman of the clean-up committee for the FFA Pancake Supper. (Dad assisted by baking pancakes.), received the Star Green Hand Award and also was a Gold Scholarship Award winner. He received a Bronze Award on the Activities Point System. FFA provided boys from the farm an opportunity to gain more expertise in farm topics, and it recognized the importance of farming to the American way of life.

Chuck also played freshman and J.V. football, was on Student Council, and worked at Wolverine in the Co-op Program. Working indoors there helped him to know that he wanted to be a farmer.

Darcia was in the top 20 out of a class of 329 in 1972. From the fourth grade through high school Dar and our cousin Sharon Porter were close friends, and they rode the bus together into high school. Dar's class was the first to have swimming as part of her P.E. course. She was also on the swim team, the only sport offered to girls at that time. Both Dar and Phyllis played trombone in the marching band.

Max Decatur, our bus driver, wrote in Phyllis's yearbook, "If all the boys and girls were as good as the ones that live on Peterson Road, we would never have any trouble." We agree.

Linda, Caroline,
Ann Pratt, 1951

Linda and Bart Ingraham,
1951

1955, 8th Grade Class: Arnold Hammer, Phyllis,
Mrs. Zigler, Ann Pratt, Jim Adams

Report of *Charles Porter*　　　Grade *3*

Progress Report

Grades 1, 2 and 3

This report card has been designed to give the parent a more complete picture of his child's progress not only in school studies, but also in the development of certain habits and attitudes which greatly influence his character and personality.

This is a check list type of report. The teacher checks the term that best describes the child's progress in the six-week term. You will be asked to come to a conference with the teacher in the first and fourth marking periods. The purpose of these conferences is that there may be a more perfect understanding of the child's needs by both parent and teacher.

Lynn H. Clark

County Superintendent of Schools

NAME *Charles Porter*

AGE

TEACHER *Margaret Connon*

SCHOOL *Courtland Center*

DATE *September, 1960*

KENT COUNTY SCHOOLS

Ron with his bike.

**Courtland Center School after it became
Courtland Township Hall, 1965.**

Courtland Center School – April 24, 1951

Chapter 6

Twice a Day—
365 Days a Year

Knowing that the cows were waiting to be milked didn't make getting out of bed any easier. The chore faced us twice a day, every day of the year, without exception. But by the time we got out the door of the house and were walking on the path toward the barn, we were resigned. We'd open the gate into the barnyard and push the red barn door along its sliding track to our left. If it was cold, the warmth from the cows' bodies would immediately strike us, and Dad always had a wide-awake greeting for us. To him, this was the best place in the world to be. We never saw him begrudge milking cows, and he never slept in—he was always on time to start milking.

As we'd stand in the open barn door and face south, we could look across the barnyard, down the lane, past the pasture and crops to the woods. Our work places and results of our labor were always in sight. Then we'd turn around and go into the barn where milking the cows was our immediate concern. Chuck says it was some of the best times he spent with Dad. The radio would be tuned to WOOD-AM where Buck Barry at 5 a.m. and Bruce Grant at 6 a.m. would accompany us as we did our chores and watched the sun rise over the pasture.

There was a routine to milking cows and a division of labor between Dad and us kids. Only one of us helped at a time, and usually it was one of the boys. First of all we would put grain in the feed alley in front of the cows' stanchions. This was usually Dad's job as he could lift the entire burlap bag and pour the appropriate amount out for each cow, while taking into account her individual milk production. We'd give them hay as well. Sometimes we'd pour molasses on the grain to entice them to eat more.

One time Ron evidently wanted a taste of molasses for himself, and he left the spigot on the barrel open. Molasses ran all over and even into the gutters. The cows' tails swished in it and spread it even further. The barn became a messy, sticky place to clean up. What happened to Ron? No one can remember.

We fed the cows silage in the winter because there was no food in the frozen pastures. The chopped up stalks of corn provided good protein for the cows and aided their four stomachs in the digestion process. The longer the silage was in the silo, the smellier and steamier it got. Sometimes it would actually ferment. Phyllis seldom did this job. However she vividly remembers one day climbing up the silo's ladder and inside to fork the silage into the cart. But when she was finished, she lost her nerve and couldn't climb back out. She tried and tried, but just couldn't get her leg over the edge of the silo and onto the ladder. So she resigned herself to spending a part of her life stuck in the silo. About that time, Dad realized that she had been gone too long, and he came to her rescue. She doesn't remember ever having that chore again.

Once the silage cart was filled, we pushed it into the barn and down the feed alley, giving each cow a forkful. (The silage fork was shaped more like a rake.) This was one of the harder jobs, as the cart was heavy and difficult to maneuver. We fed silage from late September until May when the first hay crop was ready to be harvested. Ron remembers hauling the silage in a galvanized tub for two or three cows at a time before we got the silage cart.

If it was summertime, we'd have to "get the cows" from the pasture. "Bringing them up to the barn in a thunderstorm was a frightening experience," Chuck remembers. Then we would let them into the barn and direct them into their assigned places. Until 1965 when we got free stalls with a feed bunker, each cow had a place that she was supposed to stand in. This would be determined by how much milk she gave or if she was just plain ornery or stupid and would only go into a certain stanchion. Having the grain already there was an incentive for them. Once they were in place, we'd hurry to latch the stanchion closed around their necks.

In the summer during fly season, we'd have to do "something" to keep the flies away from the cows. We put Fly Bait on the floors, and it really worked. But before that Dad used the golden-yellow flypaper strips. They were about two-inches wide by 18-inches long. He'd tack them to the ceiling of the barn in several places. Sure enough, a fly that landed on one would be stuck and would die trying to get free. Each strip could accumulate a hundred flies or more. At that point in time they looked pretty disgusting. Then they had to be taken down and replaced. Later we used liquid insecticide and hand fly sprayers. We'd spray the cow all over—sides, backs, bellies, and then we'd walk around and into the feed alley and spray their heads—to keep the flies off and keep them comfortable. Remember, contented cows give more milk.

Then we'd sweep the floors and put the straps over the cows' backs to support the milking machines. Washing their udders with warm, soapy water followed this. Next we would hand milk each teat, squirting the milk through a screen on top of a metal cup, to see if anything abnormal showed up. If there was a small chunk, it could mean mastitis. This hand milking also got them to "let their milk down," before we attached the milking machine. Only a few of the cows required "kickers," a device put on both of their rear legs to keep them from kicking the milking machine or us.

Once when Chuck was washing a cow's udder, she started kicking him. Dad had taught us to put our shoulder into the cow and push her over. But this cow continued her kicking. It was so bad, Chuck had to finally crawl out by the cow's head instead of backing out. We never saw Dad beat our cows, but he was so upset with this cow that he sold her for beef the very next day.

Dad supervised the milking machines, knowing when they were done, and pouring the milk into the stainless steel pails until Ron and Chuck were big enough to help. By then we had gone from two milkers to three and then to four milkers. A few cows gave enough milk to overflow the milking machine. Dad would dump it about half way so it didn't go up the vacuum line. He'd also try not to fill the pails too full for us kids to carry up the dirt path to the milk house. When we first started, the milk house was closer to the house.

We had milk cans that were kept in an electric milk cooler filled with cold water. If we were starting a new can, Dad would have to help, as the can would want to float and/or tip with the strainer and the milk we were pouring into it. Once a milk can was 1/3 full, we'd be on safe ground, no more tipping.

We'd watch the strainer fill up with milk, and then we'd wait for the warm, frothy liquid to empty down some more so we could add more milk. Then it'd be back down to the barn for more milk to carry to the milk house. We continued moving straps, washing cows, and carrying milk. Once the milking started, this process would be repeated over and over until all the cows were milked, about 30 cows in the 50's. The most cans we ever sent to the dairy was about 20. Think of the milkman who had to lift them, full of milk, out of the cooler. The 10-gallon cans weighed 80 to 100 pounds.

Ray Bowman was our milkman then. Ron would hear him come and run out to help him slide the cans in the insulated truck. Ray would pay him with a pint of highly, prized chocolate milk. The milk cooler was replaced with a refrigerated, bulk tank in the mid 50's.

In 1956 or '57, Dad hired Homer Baker to build a new milk house onto the barn. This was wonderful, no more carrying pails a long ways in all kinds of weather. Later the new milk house held the milk conveyor and there were no more pails of milk to carry. Dad was milking about 40-42 cows at that time. The bulk tank was first filled to overflowing in either late '65 or early '66. In 1963 Dad had bought the biggest tank of any farm around; it held 410 gallons of milk.

Somewhere during milking time, we always had to feed the barn cats. Dad would have between six and eight for which we'd fill dishes of milk. Dad had one cat, Buttons, that he could hand-squirt the milk from the cow's udder right into the cat's mouth.

Finishing the milking didn't mean the chores were over. In the wintertime we'd shake out the straw under each cow. We called this bedding them down for the night. (This was the routine until 1965 when they started using free stalls in the pole barns.) Then we fed the calves and washed the milking machines, pails, and strainer. We would also brush and curry the cows in the wintertime.

Dad would breed the cows so they'd have a calf approximately once a year. This was a way to replenish/increase his herd. They would produce milk for ten months and be dry for 60 days. Gestation time for a calf is nine months.

Feeding the calves was definitely a progressive chore. Depending upon the age of the calves, the routine varied. If they were newborns, we used galvanized pails with large white nipples sticking out of the sides near the bottom. The calves usually caught on to this routine quickly. They were fed milk/milk replacer this way for about a month. Then we taught them how to drink out of a regular pail. This could be a tedious task. It was accomplished by getting the calf to suck on our hand and then immediately putting our hand into the pail, hoping the calf would inadvertently suck up some milk. And yes, calves do have teeth!

The first week after a cow freshened (delivered her calf), we couldn't sell her milk, so it would be fed to the calves. After two weeks the calves would be given milk replacer, and at about six weeks of age, plain water. Calf pellets would be added to their menu also. We would usually hang the pails, tied with binder twine, over the posts of the pens. Along with this progression in eating ability came changes in pen location also. As they moved through the feeding variations, they would be put into a different pen. We usually had six or seven pens on the north wall of the barn.

Mother would have to routinely check Ron's pockets before washing his jeans. Somewhere along the line, while feeding calves, Ron discovered that he liked calf pellets. He would keep a supply handy in his jeans' pockets.

Mother remembers the excitement when they had their first set of twin calves. They were born in the lane during a snowstorm. They were named Frosty and Snowball. A twin heifer usually will not be a good producer, so the excitement was short-lived.

Despite the twice a day routine of milking, we liked our cows and always had our favorites. Dolly, Phyllis's first 4-H calf, was either 5th or 6th on the south side of the barn, and she'd be mad if someone got in her place. Dolly was also the cow that learned to push the barn door along its track and let herself, and whoever chose to join her, into the barn. And what a mess we'd find. The bags of grain would be ravished and their not so subtle tracks of manure would be everywhere. After discovering that it wasn't a fluke and that Dolly indeed had the gift of sliding the door open, Dad added a hook to the door. Dolly, however, was diligent in checking. Anytime after that if he forgot to hook the door, she'd work her magic and invite all her cow friends to her "grain party."

Dad's pet cow, Maizey was in the 2nd stanchion on the north side. She was the only cow that he let keep her horns because she was non-aggressive. Dad would have to get the halter and lead stubborn Emily, another 4-H cow, into her place because otherwise she wouldn't come in. Other favorite cows were Augie, Skinny, Susie, Judy, Donna, and #311, so named because that's what her number turned out to be when they started using neck chains. This was in the mid 60's, and she turned out to be one of the best cows we ever had. Dad kept her until he gave up milking, July of 1971. At this point in time, we'll also disclose a family secret: We used to name cows after Ron and Chuck's current girlfriends!

This was the routine until 1965 when the free stalls were utilized. At that time Dad was milking about 60 cows. Finishing milking by 6:10 a.m. was always the goal. There were some farmers that only started at 6 a.m., but for us, we had a big chunk of the day's work already done.

Twelve hours later, the same chores would be repeated at 4 p.m. and finished by 6 p.m. Dad never wanted us to be late to any meetings because of milking cows. We were one of the first families to get to church on Sunday nights. Until the 60's, we were the only dairy farmers at our church. Of course, it helped that we set our clocks ten minutes ahead!

Our cows were our immediate livelihood. Our lives revolved around them, their barn, their food, and their well-being. Selling Grade A milk meant that we had standards to uphold. It also meant that we never knew when "the inspector" would come by to see just how clean our barns and milk house and milking machines were. He'd either "pass" you or "write you up." This would mean that you couldn't sell Grade A milk until the problems were corrected. We always passed.

Every summer we'd have the inside of the barn white washed with a power sprayer. The cows would be afraid to come in the first few days because it was so bright. In the summer, we also would hose down the floors where the cows stood, and the gutters of the barn every day, except Sunday. (Phyllis remembers being paid 10 cents for this chore.)

Like any good business, the farm had its "consultants." Our veterinarians were essential. We used Doc Byram from Rockford and Doc Green from Belding. Our cows were given TB tests, our calves were vaccinated, and the cows were seen if they developed mastitis or milk fever. When a cow freshened, milk fever would put a cow right down. We'd have to get the vet immediately because the cow could die. The vet would put an I.V. of liquid calcium in the cow's neck because she essentially never had dried up, but had continued to produce calcium. The I.V. would have them up and on their feet almost immediately. Milk fever seemed to hit the real good producers. If the cow lived, she never seemed to return to her full production.

We also had a milk tester come once every month. This service was part of the Extension Services from MSU (Michigan State University) and the DHIA (Dairy Herd Improvement Association.) The monthly fee was $7.50 for the first ten cows and $.35 for each cow after that. The milk tester sent his information to MSU, and they in turn sent Dad the report. Our milk testers worked with approximately 26 area farmers.

Clayton Heffron always stayed overnight with us. He would test the evening's milk and the morning's milk. Each cow's milk would be weighed for production and tested for butterfat content. (This was one time when having high fat content was good! This was also the source of one of our few complaints: Dad wouldn't let us skim cream from the cans or bulk tank for whipped cream. He was certain that would be the day the milk would be tested at the dairy.) Clayton's report came to us in about one week. Dad told Chuck that it was his job to remember the cows' names for the milk tester. We kids liked it when the milk tester came because he would carry the pails of milk for Dad. When he was testing other neighbors' cows, Clayton would still stay at our house overnight—we were the only ones who had TV in the neighborhood!

Art Rosenburger was another milk tester. We liked him and his quiet ways. The Grand Rapids Press ran a photo of him and Dad looking across the pasture at our cows. Art also became a "victim" of Mother's perennial ambition of being a matchmaker. We're glad to report that in his case, she was successful. She introduced Art to Sue Van Liew, a teacher at our country school, and they celebrated their 40th anniversary in 2001. Art said, "It was always a pleasure to go to Darcy's farm. He had one of the top herds in the area. His barn was clean, and he treated his cows well. Darcy was always organized and ready for me. An added bonus was that he and Eleanor introduced me to my future wife."

Dad used a bull to breed the cows until 1958. Switching to artificial insemination was just one of Dad's innovations that made him a successful farmer. At first he used it just for his better cows, but getting rid of the bulls made all of us happy. Once Darcia was mad at Dad because the bull got loose and bred her 4-H heifer; these registered animals we wanted bred by insemination from a registered bull. The bulls could be temperamental too; Phyllis remembers being afraid as she was chased down the lane by a bull once.

Although cows were our livelihood, there were other animals on the farm that we valued as well. Border Collies became the dog of choice, as they were great help with the cattle. Our first one was Lassie, followed by Jackie, who was named after Jackie Kennedy Onassis. Dad drove 130 miles to Ann Arbor to get her.

Buttons was the matriarch of all the cats and the first one to eat. She was a black and white tiger. For many years she was a barn cat, but to everyone's surprise she later became a house cat. We had Fluffy and Snowball, a white cat that Darcia says ate her kittens once. Another favorite was Tom, a gray cat. Tom was run over as Dad backed the pickup out of the barn. That was a sad day.

We never had chickens because Mother was afraid of them. It seems that she had a rooster go after her once and peck her on the head. We did have pigs for two or three years. There were three sows and their litters. For a while there were baby pigs running all over—even getting underfoot as we hung the laundry out to dry.

Only because he loved us and because we begged did Dad buy us riding horses. This meant he had to build a separate pen. They couldn't go to pasture with the cows, as they might chase the cows and reduce the milk production. (This was always a consideration for everything we did.) Our first horse was Bessie. Dad went to an auction with Grandpa DeBoer and bought her. We think they both felt sorry for the horse—she was rather skinny. She came with a sulky so not only could we ride her, but we could also drive her. Phyllis remembers her taking off and giving a real thrill ride as she ran through the ditches pulling the sulky.

Our next horse was Ranger. He was a Tennessee Walker and a beautiful horse. After Phyllis went to college, he was sold. A couple of years later she was surprised to see Ranger while walking through the horse barns at the 4-H fair in Greenville. She stood and petted him and cried until someone asked her what was wrong. When she said that he used to be her horse, they understood.

Prince was bought for Chuck and Dar, but he became a horse that Dad actually liked. Dad bought him at Ravenna at the auction. He was black and white and sold with his saddle on. Imagine Dad's surprise when he took the saddle off to see the biggest sway back ever! Then he understood why the saddle had been included. Dad would ride Prince and even used him to herd the cows.

Cows have two end products—one is milk and the other is manure. Of course, the milk was the most valued because it brought the milk check. But the manure provided excellent fertilizer for our crops and was our contribution to ecology. Getting the manure from the barn gutters to the field wasn't a favorite task. When Dad started farming, the wheelbarrow and pitchfork were his only tools. He would clean the stalls and the gutters, recessed trenches at the tail end of the cow, and then wheel the manure out to a pile in the barnyard.

Towards the end of winter, there would be a miniature boardwalk across the barnyard from the barn to "the pile." Springtime brought the big, not to mention smelly, job of loading the manure into the manure spreader and spreading it on the fields. We looked at other farmers' barnyards and kept track of their efficiency in getting rid of their manure pile and/or how high they would let them get before spreading their manure.

A couple of years after Dad's heart attack in 1956, he had a gutter cleaner installed. It emptied the barn gutters right out to the manure spreader through a system of chain-driven metal plates. We spread manure nearly every day year-round. If the snow got too deep, it would have to be stacked for a time.

Feeding our cows and watering them were also major concerns. The water supply seemed to have more excitement because of the possible problems it posed. If it was winter and the cows were sleeping in the barn, there was always the chance of frozen pipes and a broken drinking cup. (There would be a 5 to 6-inch bowl between every two cows. If the cow would push the mechanism in the bowl down, water would come into the bowl for her to drink.) Frozen pipes and/or a stuck drinking cup could actually flood the barn.

When we first moved to the farm, there was a large concrete water tank in the barnyard. This we would fill with the garden hose. Watching the level of water to make sure it didn't run over was always "someone's" job. And if that "someone" forgot, we'd have a flooded barnyard. This meant that the cows would have to walk through mud, and that they'd track it into the barn. Not good. Later this rough cement tank was replaced by a galvanized tank, and later yet we got heated water tanks with floats—no more running over or freezing! Next to the water tanks or somewhere nearby would be the salt blocks. They were about 12-inches square and put on a stake to keep them in place. We wanted the cows to lick the salt blocks, so they'd drink more water and give more milk.

Getting our corn and oats, both of which we grew ourselves, ground into grain was a job that took place about twice a month. We would "go to mill." Dad would fill the back of the pick-up with ear corn (In 1971 we started shelling our corn as we harvested it.) and about six bags of oats. Often he would get one of us kids to hold the bags as he shoveled the oats in. At the mill he would add soybean meal, salt, and minerals. The mills that he frequented would vary. In Cedar Springs he could go to Shaws or Reimer & Eldreds. In Rockford it would be the Old Mill. In Greenville it would be Horton's. Later a portable grinder came to the farm and ground the feed for us.

These burlap bags of grain would be stored in the top of the barn on the east side. As Dad would want a certain number for each milking, he'd drop them through the trap door to the bottom level. Darcia remembers this trap door as something she was afraid of walking on when she was playing in the top of the barn. There was another trap door on the hay side of the barn that Ron should have been afraid of. Once when he was throwing hay down for the cows, he fell down too. Fortunately the bale of hay preceded him, and he landed on it. Dad was right below doing the milking, and he was really scared for Ron.

We had cows, young cattle, and calves. Some we cared for more than others. This truth became evident when Dad sent a cow that we liked to be slaughtered for our personal use. No one could eat that beef because we felt like we were eating "family." When Phyllis was at college, she received a call from home saying that her 4-H cow, Emily, had been sent for beef. Her roommate was surprised to see someone cry over a cow.

We were always proud of our herd of Holsteins. A big discussion/argument among us school-aged kids was which breed was better—Holsteins or Guernseys. We felt strongly about this issue and often debated one another. In fact, it was almost a little sad when we saw that our neighbor Ralph Pratt added some Holsteins to his Guernsey herd. There went the need for our great debating skills.

Dad had said that as soon as Dar graduated from high school, he'd quit milking cows. However, the date got moved up a year to 1971 because he didn't have much help, and he received an offer from a large dairy farmer near Greenville that he couldn't refuse. This was a good news/bad news scenario. The milk checks that had been a source of revenue for 24 years, no longer came the first and fifteenth of the month. However, the freedom from milking cows twice a day, 365 days a year was welcomed.

Dad kept all of his young cattle, the milking machines, and bulk tank in case he changed his mind. But he never did go back to milking cows. He did, however, buy and sell dairy cattle for a couple of years after that. Even though we still had the young cattle, it felt empty around the farm.

The demanding pace of the farm taught us lessons that major corporations pay experts big bucks to hopefully teach their employees. The routine of milking produced discipline in all of us. There were chores to be done, and we did our part. It also taught us teamwork. There was far too much work for one person, but divided up, it was doable. And timeliness, as adults we are still obsessed with being on time. Of course, we weren't aware of the lessons we were absorbing—at the time it just felt like WORK. Our parents were daily examples of what work ethic was all about.

1965 Christmas Card

1952. Dad with Buttercup and 1940 Ford Pickup

Dad with milk tester, Art Rosenberger
Photo was in Grand Rapids Press

Chuck taking calf to a different pen.

**Ranger, our Tennessee Walker, with
Dad, Phyllis, Dorothy Parks,
Ann Scott, Annette Burrows**

Dad, Phyllis, Ron with Margie

**Bessie, our first horse, with Phyllis and Ron.
Note cow watering tank to left.**

Chapter 7

Church at the Crossroads

Dad said he was going to drive the '57 Dodge until the wheels fell off. It was a large, black beauty of a car with big fins protruding up on either side of the trunk. Black with a white roof, it was described as being two-toned in those days. Because our lives not only revolved around the farm, but the church as well, it was only fitting that we were driving on Wabasis Lake Road, on our way to Sunday morning church, when the right, front tire literally fell off.

When we got out of the car to see what had happened, we saw the bare axle protruding out and resting on the gravel road. The wheel had popped off, and we found it in the ditch. As we pondered what to do, someone came along and gave us a ride to church. Even with our car breaking down, we were never late to church.

Growing up and working on the farm taught us our work ethic, and growing up and participating in church activities gave us our values. These principles weren't just preached to us from the pulpit, but they were demonstrated to us by the people of Oakfield Baptist Church. From Sunday school teachers to youth group leaders to our pastors, compassion was not only taught but also illustrated. We were the recipients of positive patterning long before the concept was espoused for rearing children.

Phyllis remembers Bob and Anna DeBoer taking the youth group on the church bus to "bomb" the people in Greenville. We took numerous tracts, rolled them up, and then covered them with colored, cellophane paper and twisted the ends. The finished product looked like a Tootsie Roll with flared ends. About fifteen young people boarded the bus, and Bob drove us to Greenville.

In town, we lowered the bus windows, and as Bob drove slowly up and down the streets, we threw the "bombs" to people along the sidewalks. It was sort of like throwing candy into a crowd from a parade float. But of course, we were "sending" out the good news of the Gospel, *something far greater*. And we hoped that people would be intrigued enough by the colorful missiles to unwrap them and read what was inside.

After this activity, or one similar, the DeBoers wanted to take the youth out for ice cream. Phyllis vividly remembers going to their apartment and seeing them shake their piggy bank until all the money had fallen out and then using it to buy the ice cream. The impact of that visual lesson in sacrificial giving has never diminished over the years.

As teens, we kids had Young Peoples Meetings before Sunday evening service. This was one meeting we liked and looked forward to. It was more of an informal time with us kids being given leadership opportunities. We would elect officers and do the devotions. It was a big time when we'd have officer meetings. Once Dad found out that Phyllis and her friends had been meeting in the Courtland Cemetery; he was furious. They never did that again.

Frank and Joyce Austin and our Uncle Aaron and Aunt Dee Porter were the Young People's sponsors when Chuck and Darcia attended the group. Aaron and Dee recall, "We had the young people plan and present their programs with the adults. We were trying to teach them leadership. The young people really did a good job with their responsibilities. We also planned many fun times too. We had hayrides, sledding parties, beach parties, canoeing and retreats. One retreat speaker was Dr. Duane Gish speaking on 'Creation vs. Evolution.' The kids were a really good group, and we enjoyed working with them. It makes us proud to see them following the Lord in service to this day." Darcia recalls one night at a retreat, when Aunt Dee "slept" in front of Dar's door because she had been known to sneak out and get into mischief.

As young people we could be sure that any holiday would be celebrated at church. Even proms would find their counterparts at church with a banquet for which we'd dress up and the ladies of the church would serve us. (Later these events took place at restaurants.) Halloween would often be celebrated at our house with a hayride followed by a party in the top of the barn. We'd bob for apples in the galvanized tub, try to eat marshmallows tied on string, and roast hot dogs and marshmallows over a bonfire in our ditch. Dar even decorated the grain bin into a fun/spook house.

Once Phyllis was on a hayride, just north of the church, and the sky filled with the brightest lights. It looked like 25 searchlights going all across the sky. Our first thought was that Jesus was returning to earth! One of our sponsors knew to tell us that we were seeing the Northern Lights. They were spectacular. Pam Lilly Newman recalls, "I remember that the hay wagon was approaching Oakfield Church, the ride nearly over, when someone first noticed the phenomenon. In seconds, we were all looking up as the sky blazed in multicolored, moving streaks of light. We continued gazing into the heavens after the wagon was sitting in the church parking lot. It seemed like the earth was covered with an upside-down bowl of reds, yellows, blues, and whites with a black area directly overhead. I found myself staring at the black area, thinking Jesus would appear any minute and take us up in the rapture."

Winter parties included ice-skating. Our pond, west of the barn, was one site. Dad would take bales of straw to sit on and build a fire for warmth out of wood and straw. Later Mother would serve hot chocolate with marshmallows.

Christmas was another time that our church went all out for us. We'd have a big Sunday school program with just about everyone saying a "piece." One year when Ron was four or five he had the "Welcome" to say. Needless to say, this was important because it started the whole program. By the time we got to church the whole family could say it forward and backwards because Mother had Ron practice it so much.

In addition to encouraging us to attend our own church meetings, our church also provided transportation for us to attend Youth for Christ meetings in Grand Rapids on Saturday nights. This was big time stuff for us. Ted Bryson and Dave Breese were the directors. (We had no idea that we were being influenced by men of God who went on to even greater heights. Dave Breese later became president of Taylor University, and Ted Bryson directed Maranatha Bible Conference.) Here we got a taste of a "big" God. We saw hundreds of other teenagers in a spiritual setting, and we saw that being a Christian could be FUN—more than a list of do not's. Our sights were expanded, and our hearts were quickened.

Besides our dad, there were several other bus drivers, including Bud Galantine, who drove us to YFC, and we thank them profusely for providing this glimpse into the bigger world of Christianity beyond our church and camp at Lincoln Lake. Another activity that they took us to was Hymn Sings. Various local churches would take turns once a month and invite teenagers to come and sing and enjoy special music. It was another time for us to mix and get acquainted with more youth.

Oakfield Baptist did its best to keep its young people busy and supposedly "out of trouble." The standing joke was that our list of do not's was so long that all that was left was "making out" in the back seat of the car—an activity in which probably everyone participated. One thing that was widely enjoyed was church softball games. Originally these were only for the boys; the girls came along to watch however. Dad, along with others, coached the team at one time or another. Ron could usually be found playing first base, while Chuck favored second base and shortstop. Later Dad also coached girls' softball and basketball, which Dar says was some of the best times she spent with him.

Weddings were another time that the church would be involved in our lives. If a young person from Oakfield was getting married, an invitation would be sent to the entire church. The reception would be held in the church basement. Every lady who came would bring a chocolate cake to be served along with the wedding cake. There would be nuts and mints, ice cream and punch all served by the ladies of the church. Of course, a church bridal shower would have preceded this. At times the showers would include both men and women. The church family did a great job of taking care of its own.

Our friends at church were like family. We were in their homes for sleepovers, and we'd have them over to our house. Oakfield Baptist was uniquely situated geographically at a crossroads where three school districts adjoined: Rockford, Greenville and Cedar Springs. This meant that most of our church friends were different from our school friends. This gave us a greater perspective on life. Our best friends at church were Ann Bidstrup, Ken Krause, Dan Galantine, Jon Kraus, Becky Horton, Dixie Fuller and Sharon Porter.

We all have lessons we learned and values we gained from these many encounters with the people of Oakfield Baptist Church. But it's our parents, who literally brought us up in the church, whom we thank the most. Mother first taught a Sunday school class with Ron in the baby buggy along side her. Once he threw his bottle out of the buggy onto the floor making quite a mess.

Another one of Mother's jobs was that of cradle roll. An attractive poster was kept on the wall of the narthex of the church, and each time a baby was born, a cradle with his/her name and birth date was added. Mother would call on ladies in the neighborhood who sent their older children to Sunday school and "enroll" their babies. This was done in hopes of getting the parents to come also. Material would be mailed to the homes every three months, another one of Mother's tasks.

Mother also played piano for Junior Church. This was the meeting that children through 3rd grade attended while their parents were in adult church. Some typical choruses that we sang were: "Deep and Wide," "Rolled Away," "I've Got a Home in Glory Land," "Jesus Loves Me," "Jesus Loves the Little Children," "Hallaleu," "It's Bubbling . . . in my Soul," and "He's Able." Mother could read music, but she quickly learned to play them all "by ear" also.

Mother was active in the ladies' group known as Ladies' Missionary. This group of ladies kept the church informed of their missionaries and prayed for them. Mother was a major letter writer to the missionaries, and whenever they were home and spoke in our church, Mother was usually the one who entertained them in our home. Our family especially loved having Jack and Bea Hough over. To us they WERE missions. Through the years our families' lives have been interwoven. It was Fordyce Hough who stopped and took Phyllis to Sunday school when we lived on M-57. Soon after that, Dad and Mother started attending Oakfield also. Our family supported Jack and Bea financially many years. Tom lived with our family for a year while attending high school. Jack married Chuck and Gayla. Beth lived with Phyllis and her husband Ron for a year while she attended college, and it's because of Jack and Bea that Phyllis and her husband Ron are missionaries with South America Mission. Charles and Joanne Huffstetler and Pastor Dave and Vivian Smith were often in our home also.

Bea Hough recalls, "Darcy and Eleanor were not only our supporters but our friends. Every missionary furlough, one of the first places we would head would be to their farm to fellowship with them, eating, playing games, laughing and recounting the Lord's blessing and protection upon us because they had prayed."

"One experience that I well remember was a time that we needed a vehicle. Up until this time in Peru, we had only used outboard motors on the rivers, but because of a move to a larger city, we needed a four-wheel drive vehicle. I wanted to call different supporters to make them aware of the need. Jack said, 'No, we would pray about it.' One morning Darcy called and said that the Lord had laid on their hearts the need for a vehicle for us. Not only did they buy us that vehicle, but Darcy also helped drive it to the docks in New York City for shipment to Peru. We learned later that their milk production increased that year."

Dad was also involved in various church leadership roles. He was continually a member of the Deacon Board, which oversaw the church's activities. He attended Men's Fellowship meetings, and he was Sunday School Superintendent when he wasn't teaching. He took these responsibilities seriously. In a letter written to Phyllis in 1959 he said, "Sunday is 'Teachers Day,' please pray. Sunday night we will have a teachers' meeting. We are going to glean some things from the survey you took. I think some of my teachers could leave more of a challenge."

Tuesday was calling night, and Dad was faithful. In the same letter he said, "After calling tonight, I see these families who work Sundays and have no time for the Lord. Then they end up with nothing; it just doesn't add up." In a letter dated October 1, 1959, he wrote, " I just came home from calling. I hope this letter finds you close to the Lord, then I know you too will have real joy." The letter continues, "About the calling campaign—only three of us. Last night I had prayer meeting on Why we should call, How to call, and The results if we would call and work for the Lord." He resumes, "Tonight I called on Meyers Lake Avenue north of 14 Mile Road to 16 Mile. I made 12 calls and was received in every case. Wonderful reception. Maybe 12 prospects."

Our church services started with Sunday school at 10 a.m. We'd all meet in the auditorium and sing songs, have announcements, and then be dismissed to our various classes. Our Sunday school teachers especially impacted our lives because we met in small groups. (Once Dad's class of boys met in the church bus because the space was so limited.) Not only did they teach us, but they would also take us on special outings or have parties for us. Both Ron and Chuck remember Carlton Rector. Phyllis and Dar remember Ethel Bidstrup, Iris Horton and Grace Nicholson.

Sundays at 11 a.m., we'd have church. Our sermons seemed to be more explaining Scripture rather than applying it to how we should live through the coming week. One pastor said, "We don't know much about the Holy Spirit." (But today we know that the Holy Spirit is the One who directs/helps us in our daily lives.) The emphasis seemed to be more on "being saved" than on our daily walk. Yet we saw our own parents "living" out their faith, day in and day out, and they listened to the same sermons.

Sunday evenings followed the a.m. format, but our songs wouldn't be as formal as Sunday morning. Often there'd be time for testimonies. Sometimes to pick out the next hymn to sing, we were asked to give a testimony or quote a favorite scripture. We were always hopeful that we'd hear something "exciting and new." One pastor would say, "Tonight let's share something that God has done for you *this past week*." This usually brought a memorable account.

The song leaders were important to our church life. We enjoyed Fordyce Hough and Jack Sorensen, who'd snap his fingers as he directed. Later Carl Bronkema and Larry Nicholson kept us up to tempo as we sang. Darcia especially enjoyed playing the piano while Larry was directing, and we all enjoyed the nights that we could make requests as to which songs to sing.

When it came to pastors, we all loved Pastor George Adams. He was our pastor from 1956 to 1970. His children, Paul and Kathy, were close to our ages, and his compassionate heart was an example for all our lives. Being a pastor in a small country church was a 24/7 job. People felt free to call him for just about any situation that came up. They also felt free to stop at his home—especially as it was next to the church. We never heard him complain once. Chuck remembers being home, sick in bed, and having Pastor Adams come into his bedroom and pray for him.

Wednesday evening we'd be back in church for prayer meeting. This time wasn't our favorite, but we'd go in the hopes of seeing our friends. Other families weren't as strict as ours about attending this meeting. Usually the Bakers, Hortons, Rectors and Bronkemas would be there. When the devotional was over, we would divide up to pray. We don't remember being taught to pray. The prayers we heard were usually long and boring—not relevant to kids. Some were mumbled, and we had no idea of what had been said. The absolute worst was New Year's Eve's service when we had to "pray in" the New Year.

But from our family devotions at home, we knew that prayer worked. Our parents were once again the best examples that we had. We knew that Dad and Mother often "laid out the fleece" when making important decisions. (This is based on the story of Gideon in the book of Judges.) Dad would talk to Mother and say that he would buy a cow at the auction if he could get a good one for $250. If the cow went higher, Dad would quit bidding and know that God had another cow for him to buy. He used this method in buying tractors, land, and cattle.

Thursdays were designated as F&F Clubs. This stood for Faith and Fellowship. These gatherings were mostly fun with a devotional thrown in. We had a volleyball court at the back of the parsonage, and we spent a lot of time there.

So we had four meetings on Sunday, one on Wednesday, one on Thursday, and Youth for Christ on Saturday. Yes, indeed, that left little time to "get into trouble." But just in case, we had special meetings. Sometimes they were revival meetings. This meant that a traveling evangelist who specialized in this type of ministry would be with us every night of the week. This also meant that the Porters would also

112

be in attendance. There were times that this " voice was just what we needed to pull us out of our "old" ways into a new perspective.

In a letter postmarked March 13, 1961, Mother wrote to Phyllis, "It's all real thrilling . . . . I look for great things to happen tonight. Here the closing day is so wonderful. I think the problem has been the coldness among all the members that have held back. Tears sure flowed this morning." The next day she added, "I could break some buttons, I'm so proud of my whole family. I just hope I can be a good enough Christian mother to help guide you all the right way. It's not every family that has Mother, Father, and all the children saved and living for the Lord. I think the Lord blesses us for that reason."

During the summer we'd all attend Vacation Bible School. Once again Mother was involved playing the piano and teaching a lesson. We'd fill our car full of neighborhood kids and take them with us. Of course, we in turn would go to Ashley Baptist, the Hammer's church, for their VBS and to Courtland Methodist, the Pratt's church, for their VBS. And then some years we'd also go to Grace Bible Church, our Grandma Porter and Grandma DeBoer's church, for their VBS. This summertime "church hopping" could keep a kid busy if he/she wasn't needed on the farm.

Phyllis says that VBS is where she made the most important decision in her life. The lesson was about the lost sheep and how he had strayed from the flock and the loving shepherd who went and found him and brought him safely home. The teacher said that everyone was like that sheep. The Bible says, "All we like sheep have gone astray." (Isaiah 53:6) Phyllis didn't want to be like that lost sheep, and when the time to pray came, she said her prayer out loud, sitting on the front pew. She asked Jesus to come into her heart. She told Him that she believed that He died on the cross for her sins, and that she wanted to be his child, a Christian. That was a simple prayer, and as children that's how we understand things, simply. But the ramifications of those prayers continue throughout our lives.

For the rest of the family this decision was made at home. Ron says that he was seven when he prayed with Mother. Chuck prayed with Mother in his bedroom when he was five years old. Darcia remembers praying her salvation prayer with Mom by the big, old, red sofa when she was four years old. She reaffirmed it later at Lincoln Lake Camp.

One of the highlights of VBS was plenty of time for Bible drills. The leader would have all the kids hold their Bibles up in the air. Then he'd give a Bible reference. Everyone would repeat the reference with him. When he said, "Charge," the pages would turn like fury, and the first person to locate the verse would stand and start reading it aloud. This was an activity at which we all became proficient. We were also given Bible verses to memorize and rewarded for being able to quote them. Even though the process was like "fun and games," we learned our way "around" the Bible, and to this day we can quote some of those Scripture verses.

Another summertime activity that we looked forward to was Lincoln Lake Baptist Youth Camp. We had to be eight years old to go. (Darcia went when she was seven because Phyllis was in charge of crafts and the canteen and said she'd be responsible for her; there also was an extra space available.) The first year Ron went to camp, Mother found out when she went to pick him up at the end of the week that he'd worn the same set of clothes the entire week. His new jeans had literally faded from being out in the sun so much. When Phyllis started attending camp all of the girls wore dresses, changing into pants only for the sports activity. The boys and the girls had separate swim times, and the girls could only wear one-piece bathing suits.

At this time we'd meet missionaries who would teach us an hour-long lesson every morning. Jack and Bea Hough were favorites of all of us. A favorite Bible teacher was Pastor Russ Houseman, the man who started Oakfield Baptist Church. He had big charts illustrating the end times. Besides that, the only visual aid would be the missionary slides. Phyllis remembers not liking the slides as they showed people eaten by leprosy and other horrible diseases. (Can you imagine the thoughts that flew through her mind when she and her husband later were missionaries in Liberia, West Africa, and she was introduced to a pastor who had had leprosy, and she was expected to shake his stub of a hand?)

Sports, usually softball for the guys and kick ball for the girls, would be in the afternoon, along with the craft time and then swim time. Typical crafts would be painting ceramic plaques, working with leather, and braiding lanyards. And canteen. How we loved being able to buy candy twice, every day! By the time Chuck and Dar got to camp, this was upgraded to three times, and it included ice cream.

Another highlight of camp week would be the campfire. The service would be led by one of the speakers. We'd sing "Kumbaya," and the youth would be encouraged to share testimonies. These would be accounts of trusting Jesus as Savior, of decisions to change bad behaviors, or other commitments made at camp. At the end of the service, there would often be a stack of sticks, and the opportunity was given for campers to take a stick and place it in the fire as a symbol of giving one's life to God and being willing to follow His will.

Camp was also great because of the new friends we'd make. We loved finding kids who held similar beliefs, and as we got older we always hoped to find a girlfriend or a boyfriend at camp. In 1968 Dad and Mother bought a cottage that fronted the camp swim area at Lincoln Lake. This may have helped make camp become a way of life for Darcia. Her wedding was in the camp chapel, and later she lived in an A-frame house by the camp, and she continued to work at the camp for about nine years. We'd tease her that she thought life was just a big, fun time at camp, or we'd say that she never grew up because she was still a camper—typical family banter.

One of the biggest lessons, next to our salvation, that we learned at church and saw our parents put into practice, was giving. Both of them believed that you couldn't out give God. Our church taught tithing, giving 1/10 of your income to the church, and our parents did. They gave not only their money, but also their resources. Mother even prayed that one of her children would one day be a missionary; she never told a soul until Phyllis was getting ready to board the airplane in 1978 to leave for Liberia with her family. They, and other members of Oakfield Baptist Church, truly invested their lives in their church community, all the while planning for and teaching about their real home in heaven.

"Culturally convenient rules are inevitable but must be regularly updated; moral rules must be maintained and practiced, no matter what the current culture." (Leith Anderson in *Dying for Change*) Each of us, independently, and our parents have chosen to follow this maxim. Even if our indoctrination in church was intense—all of us are worshipping today in a local church, and we have raised our children in church and at least part of the time in Christian schools.

> *Remember your leaders who spoke the word of God to you. Consider the outcome of their way of life and imitate their faith.*
>
> Hebrews 13:7, NIV

Memories from Dr. Royce Newman

Three distinct snapshots in my memory bank come to mind every time Darcy's name is mentioned:

1. When I first began attending Oakfield Baptist Church at the age of 16, Darcy was a chaperon for the boys' outing for an evening activity. We were playing basketball somewhere. I made a baseline drive and somehow made a basket. Well, Darcy talked about that event in such a way that he made me feel like I was a really good basketball player.

2. Darcy taught a Sunday school class that I was in with 6-10 other boys. We were meeting outside the church in the church bus. Darcy was one of us. He seemed to talk to us on our own level, and we would just converse with him for 5-10 minutes before the "real" lesson. There was a phrase that I can still hear him saying that would fit into many of his sentences. I believe this is a direct and accurate quote with his oft used phrase "a-goin'." "Christianity is the best thing a-goin'."

3. Darcy was not a pie-in-the-sky kind of guy. He did not view all of life through rose-colored glasses, but he was upbeat, real and practical. He illustrated trust in God by talking about his feelings of helplessness when his daughter contracted polio, and then seeing God save her life.

RELIGION *in Country Living* — By CARL STASER

"Don't close the church

I HAVE been receiving many suggestions to pass along to Mrs. Lewis. You may remember her letter that appeared in this column on February 5, 1966. She wanted suggestions for her church of 29 members that once had over 200 members.

Almost every letter says, "Don't close the church!" I believe that you will be impressed by two sample letters received recently from MICHIGAN FARMER readers. They come from dedicated persons.

After reading these two letters, I hope you will discuss them in your own home or at some church meeting. If you have some other ideas on ways to increase the effectiveness of town and country churches, please write me—Carl Staser, Michigan Farmer, Box 191, East Lansing, Michigan 48824.

• • •

Dear Mr. Staser:

In your article in the MICHIGAN FARMER concerning the "dying rural churches," we noticed that you used the picture of our church.

Our church, Oakfield Baptist, located on the corner of M 57 and Wabasis Avenue, is anything but a dying church. We have a $64,000 addition, which includes a new sanctuary to seat 400. We have a membership of 129.

Our members believe in and practice tithing to keep our church going. Last year we received $27,654.02 as our offerings. We gave $6,462.00

to missions, spent $8,917.02 on improvements (includes payments on our new sanctuary), and the rest was used for operating expenses. We have an enrollment of 200 in the Church School and 25 teachers.

We feel that the Lord blesses rural churches and we are thankful for ours. In our locality there are two other fine rural churches, the Courtland and Oakfield Methodist Churches.

I feel wherever the Word of God goes forth, regardless of rural or city localities, the Lord will bless.

We are at the present time working on a youth center with fireplace and a place for our Pioneer Girls and Boys Brigade to meet.

The people of the community gave us the former "Oakfield Chapel," which we have moved beside our church. As our members give of their time and money, we hope to be using this chapel this year. (See II Timothy 4:2)

I am enclosing a picture of how our church looks today.

Mrs. Darcy Porter
Kent County

P. S. We earn our living by farming and are regular readers of the MICHIGAN FARMER.

(Editor's Note—In preparing the religious column for our February 5 issue, we felt the message would be benefitted if we could include a picture of a rural church. We found a picture in our files we felt would be a good example and published it. Until Mrs. Porter informed us, we were not aware of the name or location of the church. Certainly we were casting no aspersions on the success or service of their church. If some of our readers are interested in sending in identified photographs of their own rural churches, from time to time we will be able to use them in our religious column.)

• • •

MARCH 19, 1966

117

Chapter 8

Four Farm Kids

We were raised to be tough and not to complain. It wasn't intentional, but that's the way it was. Dad and Mother were that way themselves. It's hard to remember them in bed because they didn't feel well. We rarely visited the doctor, and we didn't have health insurance. If we ran into the barbwire fence and our wound was bleeding a lot, we were told that was a good sign that we weren't hurt too seriously. It we fell and got hurt, but there was no blood, we were also told that was a good sign. So unless we couldn't move, see or hear, we continued on with whatever the task was before us.

One of the first chores we were given as children was mowing the grass. Keeping one's yard neatly cut was one of those "signs" of how good a farmer you were. We started out with the entire yard in front of the barn to mow plus all around the house and the back yard, with just a hand-push mower whose wheels made the blades spin. We would have to leave the hill in front of the barn for Dad; it was too strenuous for us. The back yard was often difficult to mow because of the little apples that would stop up the mower. We would use our foot to back turn the blades and then push again leaning our stomach into the handle, and off we'd go. Using the hand mower was just plain tough work.

Praise was always freely given when the job was complete. We all loved how nice it looked. Dad and Mother especially liked having the ditches mowed. We have memories of Mother whacking long grass and weeds with a scythe. For her, this was the finishing touch. Later the yard in front of the barn became partially paved over, and just when the amount of mowing was less and therefore easier, Dad bought a power lawn mower. Later he borrowed Ingraham's riding mower to see what it was like. He tried it out and immediately went into the house and ordered one over the phone. By that time we were mowing where the corncrib had been and by the tool barn.

Another chore that we'd do was to unload and stack wood for the furnace. When the pickup was backed up to the house, one of us knew we'd be asked to "throw the wood down" into the cellar. For a kid it was hard work. Backing the pickup properly was important. If Dad would get it about three feet from the opening so the tailgate would help aim the wood into the cellar, it helped us a lot.

We labeled the pieces of wood as "big," "medium" and "small." We'd pick out the small pieces and throw them down first. Next we'd get all of the medium pieces, and finally the big pieces that we could lift. The others we would try to roll to the end of the truck bed. With just the right amount of angling, we could get them to fall down. If not, they'd lie on the ground and then had to be rolled down. Sometimes we'd leave the big ones at the end of the truck for Dad. Rolling those big pieces to the end of the truck bed was hard work. But once it was off the truck, we were only half done. Then we'd go to the basement and repeat the process, only this time we would stack the wood. Our hands would be dirty, and we'd examine them for bruises and proudly point out our "badges" from unloading the wood.

We weren't "goody two-shoes;" we got into our share of trouble. Dar tipped over paint in the garage and lied to Dad saying that she didn't do it. Lying was a BIG no-no in our house, and Dad spanked her. Phyllis remembers having two or three marks on the blackboard at school for talking and getting spanked by Dad for it. Chuck remembers saying something disrespectful to Mother once. Dad got mad about it and took the keys to Chuck's car away.

Being the most curious, Ron probably had the most "incidents." We all remember that when he was four and another little boy was with him, he started up the Allis Chalmers as it sat in the top of the barn. If he'd gotten to the point of putting it into gear, they would have gone through the back of the barn, and after falling a whole story, surely would have been killed. Dad spanked him with a fan belt for that. Ron's also famous for turning off the escalator in Wurzburg's. Once he also turned on the burglar alarm in a store; Mother grabbed him and quickly walked out while the police were on their way.

4-H was a large part of our lives. Founded in 1902 to provide better agricultural education for young people, 4-H stands for Head, Heart, Hands and Health. We all had dairy as projects. Chuck was in for two years; he showed his calf, "Angel." Ron's "Daisy" placed at the end of the line, but he didn't mind because she was a top producer. Darcia showed her cow, "Emily 2" for two years. She also did vegetable gardening, flower gardening, and cooking — she made brownies. Phyllis did dairy, junior leadership, and sewing.

For sewing she made a headscarf, an apron, and darned a sock. (Remember that was the 50's.) The second year we made simple dresses. The ladies who were our leaders, Louella Markam, Elizabeth Fesaden, and Irma Becker, helped us. Supposedly this prepared us for being farm wives, but we really preferred our dairy projects. Gene Post was our dairy leader.

Getting an animal ready for the fair involved a lot of work. As soon as we chose or bought our animal, we would start taming her. We would groom her a lot by brushing, and we'd comb her tail and fluff it out. To keep her clean, we'd have her sleep with a calf blanket on. We'd also get her used to a halter by leading her all around the farmyard. We would walk backwards and direct her as she walked. When we stopped her, we wanted her front feet together and her back feet apart. This was the ideal stance. Of course, we would hold her head up too.

Before the fair, we would scrub our animal with soap and water two or three times. If we had to, we'd even use Comet on her knees or a little bit of bleach. (We always heard rumors of those who painted over dirty knees with shoe white.) A couple of weeks before the fair, Dad would get the clippers out and would clip the animal's entire head, ears, and neck to a "V" on the shoulders. This was to make the animal look sleeker as opposed to the square look of beef cattle. Then he clipped the tail, leaving the switch at the end. This we would braid and wrap to keep it clean, and then we'd fluff it out right before we went into the show ring.

For the fair we would be dressed in all white so our black and white animal would stand out and look impressive. At the last minute we'd spray her with fly spray so her coat would shine. And into the big show ring we'd go. We'd all walk our animals around the ring while the judge looked at each individual animal. He might stop us and ask questions, and then we'd continue on walking. We'd keep our eye on him all the time to see when he'd give us the "nod." Some judges were extremely subtle while others would boldly point at us and tell us where to line up our animals.

Of course, we wanted to be placed near the top of the line. We showed Holsteins, and they always had the most competition. In fact, it was so tough that placing in the top third was considered very good. The time that Phyllis brought home the Grand Champion ribbon with her Emily was indeed a time for celebration. And later they went to Michigan State University for the statewide competition. (Ralph Pratt took Emily to East Lansing, and Uncle Aaron and Aunt Dee took Phyllis, as Dad was laid up with his heart attack.) 4-H made us farm kids proud of our accomplishments and our farm heritage.

Even though we were growing up on a farm, Mother made sure we had some culture in our lives. All of us except Ron took piano lessons. Chuck once played a duet with Dar when they attended Lakes Elementary. Iris Horton was their music teacher. Phyllis and Dar both played trombone in the Rockford High marching band. Darcia is the one who really inherited Mother's musical genes and went on to play in church and for special events. To this day she plays a keyboard in a Praise Band at her church.

We may have been raised to be tough, but we didn't escape the usual childhood diseases. While still living on M-57, Phyllis and Ron caught the measles and broke out with little red spots. Mother kept the shades pulled as the light was supposedly harmful to our eyes. On Petersen, when Phyllis was nine and Ron was five, we came down with the mumps. They were painful. We swelled out so much that we didn't have a neck. The only comfort we could get was to take dishtowels, lay them on the register to warm up, and then wrap them around our necks. Mumps lasted seven to ten days, and if you only had them on one side, you could get them again. We all had chickenpox.

If we had colds, Vicks was the main source of comfort. We'd rub our chests with Vicks and then cover it with a towel warmed on the register and go to bed. If we were coughing in the night, Dad would come with a spoonful of butter and honey. It worked. For routine cuts and bruises there were Merthiolate or Mecurochrome and Iodine. They were similar, except Iodine stung like crazy, and we'd blow on our wound so the sting wasn't as bad. Both came in a small, square, glass bottle about 3/4 of an inch in diameter and 2 1/2 inches high. Instead of a cap there was a rubber stopper with a glass dauber with which the liquid would be applied. Merthiolate was pinkish; Iodine was yellow and would stain. We didn't especially like them, but they were all we had.

One nice thing about having a big farmhouse was that we had our own bedroom. Most of us played bedroom roulette, but Ron always had the same small room upstairs. We remember him declaring that his favorite colors were green, brown and orange. Chuck did the most floating: he was in the room off the living room when he was young, then the room by the bathroom, and then back to the first one. Darcia also had the small bedroom off the living room, but then moved to the big bedroom upstairs. She remembers painting her furniture red with antique staining. Phyllis started in the small bedroom off the living room. She remembers having hand-me-downs from cousin Kay of a striped blue and white bedspread with a matching curtain and a vanity with the same blue and white skirt.

In the 50's the home economics teacher from Rockford High made home visits. Miss Blazer must have liked Mother's house and Phyllis's coordinated bedroom. She made a whole field trip out of bringing all the girls on the bus to see the bedroom. Mother served snacks, and Phyllis was labeled the girl with THE bedroom. Later Phyllis moved to the large bedroom upstairs.

Phyllis and Dar both remember liking to go into Mother's bedroom to sit on the bench of her vanity. It had a big, round mirror and lots of drawers. We'd try on her jewelry and pretend to be older than we were. Dar would also get into Mother's powder and sneak squirts of her perfume.

Without knowing all the psychology about the importance of a father/daughter relationship, Dad did all the right things. He would hug us and kiss us and tell us that we looked nice. He always told us we did a good job. Darcia remembers that each time after she played the piano that he would tell her that she had played the piano the best ever. Dar also remembers always getting a new dress for Easter.

We grew up receiving love from both parents. It surely must have stretched them out of their comfort zones, as that's not how they were raised. Phyllis remembers going with Mother to visit Grandpa DeBoer near the end of his life. That day he told Mother that he loved her. Later in the car, through her tears, she said that was the first time he had ever told her that. Perhaps one of the best things our parents did for us was to be free in showing affection towards each other. We were never surprised to see Dad come into the house at noon and greet Mother with a big hug and a kiss. Sometimes he'd embrace her a little too long, and she'd say, "Darcy...."

We all agree that growing up on the farm taught us values and discipline for life. Looking back we appreciate learning to work and being able to work closely with our parents. We also knew our neighbors and admired them. (Ron wanted bib overalls, which he called his "Dayton" [Hammer] pants. Dayton was always friendly to us kids; we liked his smile and the way he talked so fast. Dorcas was known for her wonderful homemade bread and pies. She'd make pineapple pie if she knew that Dad would be eating there. And we kids loved to hear her say, "Oh my conscience.") We learned to take pride in our work and family. The boys learned how to operate machinery, and by example, we all learned how to manage money. And we valued animals long before the need for the ASPCA.

The downside? Not much free time, and we always had to be home by 4 p.m. Only one bathroom for a family of six often posed problems too. Chuck thought that the worst jobs were cleaning calf pens and cleaning the barn after milking a cow that had just kicked you. Scraping manure off the barnyard was another least favorite chore.

Our fears were related to the times. We feared that the Russians/ Communists would come take over our country. We never knew when someone might be spying on us or trying to subvert our thinking. One family in our church even built a bomb shelter, and the Community Club at school saw a Civil Defense Film on what to do in case of an atomic bomb attack. In spite of this, we never had a house key and never locked the house until Linda Ingraham Filkins was murdered. Then we had a lock put on.

To a much lesser degree, our electric fence frightened Phyllis. Once she took a hold of it to crawl through or under, not knowing that the power was turned on, and she got a shock that went through her whole body and ended in her right leg at the site of her foot surgery.

Not all of our work was done on our farm. Potato picking time was great for earning extra money. Pratts and Thompsons raised potatoes. Even Mother would pick up potatoes. We used a crate made of wooden slats and positioned it between two rows and sorted the potatoes out from the stems and dirt and threw them into the crates. (Mother would have to yell at Ron because after he'd earned a dollar, he would throw the potatoes. Those little ones about an inch round would sting like crazy too!) If we picked up potatoes with another person, we'd cover four rows at a time. As the crates would get full, they'd also get heavy. We'd push or pull them between the rows and have to get help when they were almost full. We'd try to round up the tops to show we did a good job.

When we'd get ten crates filled, we'd mark them with a clump of vines so we could keep track of how many we had picked. Some people would actually keep track on a little note pad. All along we'd be figuring how much money we'd made by multiplying in our heads. The average rate was 8¢ a crate. If a farmer was paying 10 or 11¢, the highest that we can remember, one would wonder if his crop wasn't too good, and if we'd have to cover more territory to get a crate full.

It wasn't a lot of money, but it all added up. Ann Pratt remembers earning $18.00 one year picking potatoes for her Dad. Wurzburg's had a sale, and she wanted a bike that was $38.98. Her folks put up the rest of the money, and the blue and white bike was delivered to their farm. (Girls generally had blue bikes and boys had red ones.)

Other work away from the farm was mostly for the girls. Phyllis remembers ironing for Grandma DeBoer, doing housework for Aunt Zelma, and babysitting for Ingrahams. Darcia cleaned house and babysat for Ann Pratt Scott, who at the time was living in her family's farmhouse.

127

Ron and Chuck worked the hardest on the farm, and they received the most immediate rewards. They both had their first cars before they turned 16, and they usually had money in their pockets. Ron was 15 when he got a '55 Ford. Two weeks before he turned 16, Chuck got a 1968 Mustang. Darcia got a Ford Fairlane for $400 when she was 16. It had a broken spring and tilted to the left all the time. Phyllis didn't get a car of her own until she graduated from college, but it was a brand, new 1963 Dodge Dart.

Being part of a family business was like paddling a canoe down the river. There were times we sat in the bow (front), enjoyed the scenery, and put our oar in when the person in the stern (back) directed us to. This was usually over the fast parts and/or when there were rocks to avoid.

As kids on the farm we started in the middle of the canoe with no paddle. We enjoyed the scenery of the trip, wondered when we'd "get there," and had the time to enjoy being with our elders and observing them. It all looked like fun, and we wanted a position with a paddle badly.

The first time we were given the paddle and allowed to be the front person was exciting. We got to do a "big person" chore, and it usually ended with praise. But when the river flowed fast and up and over the rocks, we also experienced the tenseness and the responsibility of keeping the canoe on course.

The girls on the farm started as passengers and only worked their way to the front "helper" position. We assisted with milking, washing the milking machines and bulk tank, driving the tractor at haying season, and maybe some dragging, and mowing the yard and washing the trucks and cars.

But the boys on the farm had to make the transition from passenger to helper much sooner than the girls. And then before they knew it, they were sitting in the back of the canoe doing the hard jobs. For them the thrill of the canoe trip waned long before the trip was over. Sitting in the all-consuming navigation seats too often and not determining the "destination" like our parents did, the once pleasurable trip quickly went from fun to the feeling of just plain work. And the more canoes that the family put into the water, it became easy for them to want to be in control of their own destiny.

In our family, the boys responded to this differently. Their transition from hired hands to getting away from the farm completely, to returning to farm life was similar even though separated by several years. Ron joined the Air Force two months out of high school in 1963. (Dad and Mother had to sign for him, as he was only 17.) Chuck went to Michigan State University to study agriculture production and beef, but after one year he returned home to help on the farm and to get married.

Upon his return, Chuck went back to work for Dad full-time until 1975. In 1973 he bought his own farm on Whittall Road. Ron returned to the farm in 1966 and worked for Dad a year and a half. In 1970 he purchased a farm nearby on 12 Mile Road. Dad helped them both get started by letting them use some of his farm equipment, but they never entered into a family partnership. They became men just like Dad: hard working and independent.

Ron was the ring bearer in six weddings.

Ron, Chuck and Dar, 1957

Chuck and Darcia 1955

Phyllis, Ron and Chuck at Aunt Crystal's

June 1956 in front of the spirea bushes

Darcia with Emily #2, 1964

**Phyllis and Emily at Michigan State
University, 1956**

Picking pussy willows down by the creek.

Chapter 9

Many Lives,
Many Hands . . .

Dad and Mother never could have succeeded with a farm the size that they were finally running without the help of several more people than us kids. By 1970 Dad was farming 400 acres and milking 60 cows. Even when Ron and Chuck were working fulltime for him, harvest season would bring the need for more help.

We had a few hired men who came and lived with us. Percy was a happy, hard-working, knowledgeable man, but he was also a little strange. One day you'd look up and he would be gone. In a couple of days, we'd get a phone call from his current place of employment asking if they could bring him to get his things. And then again in six months, he'd show up at our farm, and Mother would be making the phone call to his past employer about picking up his things. Dad was always glad to see him return. But the time finally came when Dad said, "This is the last time. If Percy leaves again, he's not coming back," and he didn't.

Walter Eckley came when Dad had his heart attack and stayed for about a year. Walter was also hard working and capable. He helped our family out when we were in a tight spot. Walter was a younger, quiet man and fit into our way of life easily. One evening after supper, Phyllis was looking for some fun and saw Ron sitting in a chair in the living room reading the newspaper. Well, she backed up to the arm of the chair, propelled herself onto his lap, crushing the newspaper, only to find out that it was Walter! She says that was the most embarrassing time of her life.

We couldn't remember the names of everyone who helped on the farm, but we did recall some. Cousins who worked on the farm at one time or another were Louie Johnson, Milt Ammerman, and Lyle DeBoer. Neighbors who helped were Dave Becker, Paul Becker, Claire Allen, and Mel Hoekstra. From church there were Larry and Tom Nicholson. These hired hands did mostly seasonal labor during various harvests. Louie said, "Darcy was easy to work with. He never yelled or got mad and never would ask me to do something he wouldn't do himself." When he came into the house at mealtime, Louie would tease Mother by going to the stove and lifting all the covers off the pans while asking, "What are we having to eat?"

Three others came to live with us for a period of time, but not as hired men. Cousin Ray Morris lived with us six months to a year after Aunt Zelma, his mother, married Uncle Bob Hansen. She couldn't handle him at that time. Sam Pell lived with us a year or two after his father, Phil, married our Aunt Reva Ammerman. Tom Hough lived with us so he could attend Rockford High School his junior year. His parents, Jack and Bea, were missionaries in Peru and not due home for furlough for a year. When Tom first came, he went barefoot all the time. Mother was afraid that she wouldn't be able to get him to wear shoes when school started, but he did.

Tom recalls, "I went through big changes in culture after growing up for seventeen years along the headwaters of the Amazon in South America and then going to rural U.S.A. Given the nickname of 'Gringo,' I was accepted as one of the family with the Porters; they are 'my family' to this day. Darcy and Eleanor nurtured me daily with love and discipline that helped me overcome my fears and uncertainty in high school, in the city, at church, and on the farm. Darcy became a hero to me with his example of being a Godly man, husband, and father. Ron, Chuck, and Dar became brothers and sister to me. I will forever cherish the memories of being a 'Porter.'"

Whoever was eating supper with us also was there for family devotions. Dad wouldn't let us skip. Usually he'd read the Daily Bread. When it was just our family, he'd alternate days for the boys and the girls to pray. When Phyllis and Ron were gone, Dad and

Mother got Chuck and Dar to memorize Psalm 23 and Psalm 100. They were paid a dollar once they could say the whole passage. This wasn't the only time that Dad would pray. Chuck remembers Dad praying for wisdom while working on Chuck's corn dryer at 6:30 a.m.

Before Chuck and Dar were born, we had a couple and their son rent the upstairs for almost a year. He was a pipe liner, bringing natural gas from Alaska, we think.

The farm was a place that our city relatives would come to get sweet corn or to show their children what a farm was like. For about seven years, Forrest Roosa, Rockford Junior High School's guidance counselor, would bring a busload of 25 to 30 students to visit the farm. The teachers would try to milk a cow. The kids loved it; they'd never been to a farm. Forrest said, "Darcy would answer all kinds of questions. 'What time do cows get us?' 'Who gets them up?' 'What time do they go to bed?' Mr. and Mrs. Porter were a gracious host and hostesses. After visiting the barn, we'd go to the farmhouse. Eleanor would let them look all around. Once we went in the fall, and she served them all apple cider and home made donuts. They were delicious. Usually we'd go in the spring, and she'd serve hot chocolate and cookies. It was a definite highlight for the students and for me."

Our grandparents were important to us. Phyllis has the most memories of Grandpa and Grandma DeBoer. She was the oldest grandchild and the only one who called them "Dad" and "Ma." She often stayed at their house overnight. "Ma" taught her how to embroider and how to play Chinese checkers. She also made her pineapple pie and cookies with pineapple in them. When she was 75, Grandma De Boer wrote a book about Michigan history that went on to several printings. Dar remembers sitting on her porch and playing a game of counting the cars that went by and/or the different colors. (Peterson Rd. didn't have much traffic.) Chuck remembers their arguing, but says that their stories were fun to listen to. Ron thought that Grandpa John was great! Grandpa was so proud of his Dutch heritage that he took personal offense at Hollander jokes.

Our memories of Grandma Porter are mostly when she lived in an apartment in Rockford. Chuck and Dar would go there sometimes after junior high school and stay until Mother would pick them up.

They loved walking on the sidewalks downtown to buy candy. On different occasions they would stay overnight with her. One of the cool, scariest things was that Grandma Porter lived across from the funeral home, and it happened that Grandma was Dave Pederson's first funeral in Rockford. Phyllis remembers her pretty dish that she always kept crackers in and is pleased to now have it in her own china cabinet. Darcia has her little box of Scripture cards that she would read at mealtime. Ron says, "She was a saint!"

Grandpa Porter passed away in 1952. Instead of taking his body to the funeral home, it was kept at home. This was probably one of the last deaths handled that way.

Great Grandpa DeBoer lived to be 91-years old. When Phyllis had her two boys, Fred and Tom, in 1967 and 69, they became the fifth generation. There was an article with a photo in the local newspaper. Great Grandpa told Phyllis, "When you reach 90, it's lonely, as all your friends are gone." Chuck remembers him as a nice, easy-going man.

One couldn't be a recluse and be a farmer. Our lives touched and were touched by many special people. These relationships enriched us and made us well-rounded individuals. Perhaps that's why travel isn't all that important to a farmer, for he touches the world almost every day.

Some people come into our lives and quickly go.
Some stay for a while and leave footprints on our hearts.
And we are never, ever the same.

—Author Unknown

Five Generations, 1969

Five Generations, 1967

**Grandpa and
Grandma Porter**

Grandpa and Grandma DeBoer

Chapter 10

Horse Races and Cow Tipping

Remembering life on the farm, our first thoughts are of the work we did. However, after putting our minds to it, we recalled a lot of things we did for fun. Using our imagination was at the top of the list. Of course, the younger we were, the more time we had for playtime.

The top of the barn provided us with a plethora of sites to play. The opportunities for creativity and pretending were endless. It was also close by and easily accessible. The oat bin was just plain fun to climb into and try to walk around without sinking too deep into the oats. Dad was always leery of us doing this; he was afraid that we'd inadvertently get buried in the oats. Next to the oat bin was an open area, more or less, that we'd make into a playhouse. That was, if it wasn't full of bags of grain. That's where the trap door for throwing the grain down to the cow barn was.

Then there was the straw mow above the oat bin and the grain storage area. Climbing up the crude ladder that was nailed against the wall was in itself quite a challenge. There was no space to put the balls of our feet firmly on the ladder rungs—we could only use our toes on the one-inch flat rung. At the top, we'd have to either keep going right up and over the ladder or angle ourselves around the side and kind of jump to the floor. Once we got up there, we would rearrange the bales and play house. Most of the time it was the highest point in the barn, unless the haymow was filled to capacity, and exciting just because of its height.

The haymow took up most of the barn floor, and its aroma permeated the whole top of the barn—like fresh cut grass, but more pungent. The challenge of climbing to the top was always calling us. It was difficult. The bales made big steps, and if the bales hadn't been stacked tightly against each other, there was always the risk of falling into a "hole." Dad didn't like us to play there too much either because of our own safety and because he didn't want the bales broken apart. We had a rope swing for a while, but Hammers had the best rope swing in their barn, and they also had a good place to play basketball.

Another part of the barn that we used for play was the hill that went up to the large, front doors. The barn was built like a walkout ranch building with two-stories to the back and only one to the front. We learned how to ride our two-wheeled bikes by starting at the top of the hill and trying to keep upright by first coasting and then pedaling our way down. After a few crashes on the lawn, we could usually ride.

Sometimes we'd just lie down on the grass and roll down the hill. It would work the best if you would keep your arms parallel with your body and not raise your head. We'd see who could roll the furthest. Being heavier helped here, but not always. Some days a good roll down the hill just made a kid feel good. In the wintertime, we'd use the hill for sledding. After we got the big round "saucers," it could become a thrill ride. We could make runs down either side of the hill or straight down the front.

(Dad also used the hill to load cattle. He would lower the tailgate of the pickup and back up to the hill until the box just touched the hill. Then he'd lead the cow up the hill and part way back down into the rear of the pickup. Then he'd tie her rope to the front of the box, drive the truck forward so he could close the tailgate, and proceed to his destination. Sometimes he'd use two ropes to secure the cow's head, just to make sure she didn't get loose and hurt herself.)

Chuck used the yard by the barn to hit the softball against the barn wall and roof. Then he'd practice catching the ball as it returned to him. Yes, he broke the window, and then he'd have to tell Dad, but Dad didn't get too mad.

If the cows were in the barnyard and lying down, we'd have fun climbing onto their backs and seeing if we could stay on while they stood up. And they always would. (A cow has a bony backbone and there's nothing to hang onto!) First she would get up on her knees, and we could usually stay on through that process. Next she'd straighten out her back legs, and if we were still on, the cow's back would be at a steep angle heading towards the ground from the rear down to her head. This was the most difficult part! We'd usually tumble off over the cow's head, and hopefully not land in a "cow flop." The third part was when she'd completely unfold her front legs to her full height. If we were still on, we'd both be surprised. Of course, we choose only the tame cows to try this out on, because we didn't want a bucking ride around the barnyard. This was another activity that Dad frowned on, because he didn't want us to scare the cows and make them hold back their milk.

We also liked to climb trees. Our favorite tree to climb was between the house and milk house by the driveway. However, we had to remove it because it was in the way of the milk truck. Because Dad felt bad for us, he nailed some wood, like a ladder, onto one of the large Maple trees near the house. Ron's favorite tree was the apple tree by the sand pile; we had a tire swing hanging from that tree.

We could always walk back to the woods and explore an old dump. We would usually do this with a friend. Then there was the creek. It, too, would call our names to stop and play. On the way home from school, it was a good place to stop and rest before we had to ride our bikes up the hill to our farm. In the springtime it'd be full of water; it's a wonder we didn't drown. We'd try to walk across it on rocks, and once we found a huge board that fit across the creek. One by one we (Phyllis, Ann Pratt, Bonnie and Jeannie Cavanaugh) got on the board and sat down. We were all on it and bouncing a little bit, when it cracked and split in half. We fell into the creek laughing and got all wet.

We'd throw stones at frogs, always thinking that we'd get a frogs' leg dinner. Only once did we ever have enough for Mother to fry in butter. We were luckier when it came to finding morels (mushrooms). If Dad found some, he'd bring them home like trophies. They were delicious fried in butter. (Mother fried and cooked everything with butter.)

When Chuck and Dar were toddlers, Phyllis and Ann Pratt would play with them like they were big dolls. We'd push them around the yard in a doll buggy and give them rides in our bike baskets. Sometimes we'd dress Chuck up as a girl and take his picture. Since we were always playing house, they provided us hours of entertainment and gave Mother time alone in the house. We also spent a lot of time in our attic playing house.

The front bedroom had a long closet—about 10 feet by 3 feet. It was a perfect place to turn into a "house." A lot of playtime was spent there. We had a little red cupboard with glass doors in which we kept our play dishes. It had been Mother's gift from her Grandma DeBoer. We also had a red doll cradle that Uncle Arthur made for Phyllis in shop class. And we had a lot of imagination and a lot of pretending which we also used with our paper dolls. We'd carefully cut the dolls out from the cardboard cover of the 12" x 18" book, and then we'd cut the clothes from the inside pages. The clothes came with tabs, which we'd fold down to keep the dresses on our dolls. We girls became very good cutters of paper dolls. By the time Darcia played with paper dolls, they came with serrated edges, and she could carefully punch and/or rip them out.

Mother's favorite flower was the hollyhock, but we girls knew that it also made the best flower ladies. We'd pick off a blossom that was in full bloom, and that would be our lady's skirt. Then we'd find one the same color that was budding enough to show the color. We'd take that bud off, being careful to leave some stem. We'd stick that stem in one of the "holes" near the top of the "skirt" stem, sit it down with the flare of the skirt as the base, and *viola*, a flower lady. We'd also take the stems from dandelions and attach them together by sticking a smaller stem into a bigger stem until we had necklaces.

Chuck had a clown doll, Billy, that we all thought was wonderful; when you pinched its bottom the eyes would light up. This was quite a novelty to us. Phyllis had a collection of miniature dolls from different countries bought at a grocery store for $2 to $3 if we bought a certain amount of groceries. Relatives saved their grocery receipts for Phyllis. Chuck had a baseball card collection that included Pete Rose's rookie card, Willie Mays and Micky Mantle cards and other 60's stars. Chuck and Dar both had marble collections. Ron made model cars from kits. Darcia had the first Barbie dolls that came out and the Barbie Dream House. One of the bus drivers liked Dar so much that she made Barbie doll clothes for her.

Ron and Chuck had a collection of Farm-all and International toy tractors and farm equipment. They'd play farm with shelled corn. Chuck used to pretend he was talking to Dayton Hammer in the field. We also had a metal barn and a metal dollhouse.

Riding horseback was fun, especially when all of us neighbor kids would get our horses out at the same time. Unfortunately, that didn't happen very often, but we did all ride them to school once. One of our highlights was playing with the Hammers and getting their horse, Prince, up the hill to our house. This took awhile as he didn't want to come. We had to lead/pull him. Once we got him to our house, two of us would get on his back, and without any urging he'd RUN down the hill back to his home. He didn't slow up for Hammer's driveway, or going into the barn, or around the corner into his stall either. He didn't put on his brakes and stop until he was in his stall. If we were still on his back, we'd have to wait for our breath to return before we could enjoy the thrill of the ride. Then we would do it again! Prince was the fastest horse, especially if he was heading towards home.

When we were young, like most kids, the house was our main place to play. Because of their closeness in age, Chuck and Dar were probably the only siblings that actually played together, and Darcia usually got the short end of the stick. Chuck would play house with Dar for one hour and then Dar would play farm with him for two to three hours. Once when they were playing cowboys and Indians, Chuck tied Darcia to the leg of the piano and left her there while he went on to something else. When Mother found what had happened, she took their picture.

Outside Dad made a sand pile in a big, old tractor tire. It kept the sand confined and gave us a place to sit while we played. Phyllis would make mud pies and tell Ron that they were real and tasted like chocolate. Sometimes she'd cut up little green apples from the tree by the sand pile and put them on top. Apparently he was always hopeful that they would taste good, because he sampled them on more than one occasion. (Our sand wasn't white, hence the dark looking pies.)

Playing games kept us entertained, either with our friends or family members. We'd play Pick-up-sticks, Monopoly, Rook, Caroms, Chinese Checkers and a home-made game of pitching rubber jar rings at large hooks next to numbers screwed into a diamond-shaped board. But the family favorite was Rook! We could play it with our eyes closed and at a young age. We played Rook at home and at school.

Ron got a B-B gun when he was 10 or 12 and a 22 rifle when he was 16. Chuck also got his B-B gun when he was 10 and his 22 rifle when he was 15. Our family itself wasn't big on hunting, but we regularly had cousins come out and hunt on our farm. They'd get rabbits, squirrels, and deer. Dad always wanted them to be careful and not shoot a cow.

Reading material that came into our home on a regular basis was *The Grand Rapids Press, Farm Journal, Michigan Farmer, Prairie Farmer, Successful Farming*, and the *Rockford Register*. The Press came in the mail, and we read it at night. The Sears and Penney's catalogs were favorites of us kids. Mother used to read Uncle Wiggily (See Appendix) to Phyllis and Ron from the Press. Sometimes we'd act it out. Dad would be the bobcat and put a blanket over his head and try to catch us. We'd scream and run to Mother, who was Uncle Wiggily, to save us. Mother also wrote a column for the *Rockford Register* for three or four years. It was called Courtland Clippings, and it contained the "social" events of the neighborhood. (See Appendix) She was paid $.10/inch and usually got $3 to $4/week.

In the '60's Mother purchased the World Book Encyclopedia for Chuck and Dar. She paid the payments out of her grocery money. When it was half paid for, Dad told her to write a check and pay off the balance. For a long time Phyllis received *Jack and Jill* magazine from Grandma DeBoer.

If Mother was coaxed at all by Dad, she'd play the piano for us. Dad never requested church songs; he would start by asking for the "Beer Barrel Polka" and proceed to other WWII favorites such as "Rosie the Riveter," "Blue Skirt Walk" "On Mockingbird Hill" "The Five Minute Waltz" and "Red Wing."

Listening to the radio wasn't high on our list of our activities. It was something that Dad had on in the barn, and we listened to it in the car. We do remember stretching our imagination as we listened to "The Shadow." We enjoyed "Amos & Andy," and Dad listened to Gabriel Heatter and the news.

Courtland Center Community Club was a social event that parents and students alike looked forward to. It met every month. One of their fundraisers was the Box Social. The women would fill a shoebox with homemade food and then wrap it up and decorate it, usually with crepe paper, thin wrinkled paper that could be stretched. No names would be attached to the boxes; this way the food inside would be a surprise, plus the dinner companion. Then the men would bid and eat the lunch with the lady whose box it was. Dad always made the highest bid, usually about $10. Once Mother had to share hers with two men: Dayton Hammer and Ralph Pratt. (Knowing Mother, there was probably enough food too.) One time Ron bid the highest for the students' auction because it belonged to Carolyn Pratt. We would always try to find out which box belonged to whom and pass the word.

Another activity would be the Spelling Bee. Adults would line up around the room and be given words to spell. The last one standing was the winner. Mother was a terrific speller and would be one of the last ones standing. As we watched the adults quickly spell out of the circle, we kids understood why some of our classmates had difficulty with their spelling.

We'd also see our neighbors on Saturday nights in Cedar Springs. We'd walk up and down the sidewalks. We kids would go in the 5 & 10¢ store and wander up and down each aisle. The first items would truly be 5¢ and then would come the 10¢ items. The further down the aisle we'd go, the higher the prices would be. We could buy a candy bar, five suckers or a pack of gum for 5¢ (Black Jack gum was black and tasted like licorice.), or at the dairy bar we could get a single dip ice cream cone for 5¢. Notebook paper for school was 10¢. The men would usually linger on the street talking to their neighbors. The women would sit in their cars and look at people. It was truly a time when life moved slower.

Sunday afternoons we would go visiting. We didn't call ahead; we'd just show up. If the relatives weren't home, we'd leave a note saying that we'd stopped by. This was as good as a visit, and the social obligation to return the call then rested on them. If we stayed home, Mother had to be prepared to entertain, because usually someone would come to see us. We saw our aunts and uncles a lot more in the 50's than in the 60's when times got busier and people had TV's!

One night in '52 while Dad was milking cows, he decided that he was going to buy a TV. He and Mother went to John Koennes in Cedar Springs and returned with a Motorola TV. It had a 16-inch monitor in a mahogany cabinet. Mother had to arrange the living room so every seat had a good view. We were told not to sit too close because it would hurt our eyes because of radiation from the TV. She also filled the empty spaces along the wall with chairs from the dining room, as everyone came to see the TV! Ours was the first one in the neighborhood.

People didn't make any pretense—they didn't come to chat or be neighborly—they came to see the TV. Mother would usually serve coffee and dessert. They'd sit and watch "The Texaco Star Theater with Milton Berle," "You Bet Your Life with Groucho Marx," or "Ted Mack's Original Amateur Hour," and some stayed so late, that Dad would just go to bed, as he had to get up at 4 a.m. to milk the cows. Our friends would come over after school. We'd get disgusted because they'd want to watch "Howdy Doody" and the "Mickey Mouse Club" instead of playing. TV didn't even come on until 4 p.m. We'd sit there and stare at the test pattern until Kate Smith appeared singing, "When the Moon Comes Over the Mountain." We kids didn't care for her at all, but "Howdy Doody" held our attention as did "Bozo the Clown," "Rin Tin Tin," "Hopalong Cassidy,""Gabby Hayes," "Kukla, Fran and Ollie," "Buck Barry," and "The Lone Ranger." We would beg to be allowed to stay up late and watch "I Love Lucy," which came on at 9 p.m.

Chuck and Dar were on Romper Room, a preschool program that originated in Grand Rapids. Miss Jean would look in her magic mirror and greet children by name. Everyone would listen closely, hoping to hear his/her name as Miss Jean said good-bye for the day. We weren't allowed to watch TV on Sunday for many years, but when Chuck developed an interest in sports, Dad changed the rule.

Also on Sundays, while Mother was preparing dinner, Dad would play Dollar with us kids. A fly ball caught was a dollar; a hit on the ground was 25¢. If it had two bounces it was 50¢ and one bounce 75¢. When you got $3 or $5, it was your turn to bat. After dinner, Dad would take Chuck and Dar for walks in the woods or at the farms on 12 Mile Road.

Even though we had to be home by 4 p.m. to milk the cows, holidays were usually a day off from regular work. Memorial Day, we called it Decoration Day, would find us at the cemetery. The week prior, Mother would put flowers on the family graves. She would usually do Grandpa Porter's at Courtland Cemetery (at the end of Peterson Road) and sometimes help Grandma DeBoer do the graves in the Rockford Cemetery. It was very important in our family that we show respect for the deceased. On Memorial Day we'd go to the Courtland Cemetery for the Memorial Service. There would be a short devotional and then the horns would play taps. When Dad was township supervisor, he would be one of the speakers. Afterward we'd walk around reading the various tombstones, always being careful where we stepped, as it was wrong to step on the actual grave. After this we'd have a picnic.

Sometimes on July 4 we would drive to Lake Michigan with Bidstrups and/or Rectors for a picnic. This would be great fun for us. Phyllis remembers Dad stopping and buying a huge watermelon for $1. We thought that was a great treat. We loved the white sand of the beaches and the waves of the lake. The water was usually freezing cold, but we'd go in and play anyway. Our fun would be short-lived however, as we had to be home by 4 p.m. to milk the cows. After the chores were over and after dark, we'd drive to see fireworks. This would usually be to a hill nearby. Sparklers were purchased for us kids to enjoy. Not until Ron got older did we have firecrackers.

Another treat would be to drive to the Grand Rapids Airport and hopefully see an airplane arrive or take off. We'd pull up and park and patiently wait. Many times, after an hour, we'd have to leave without seeing one.

Uncle Gary and Aunt Emily DeBoer didn't have any children, but they had a huge house on Tiffany Ave. We'd go there for Thanksgiving dinner. We'd have 20 people. Phyllis loved this event, as it was the only time she had cousins her age to play with: Sally and Nancy Cavanaugh. Great Grandpa DeBoer would be there, Uncle Ben and Aunt Tina Den Braber with Elmer and Ed, Aunt Anna and Uncle Jack Cavanaugh, Grandpa and Grandma De Boer and Uncle Gaylord and Lyle.

When Great Grandpa married Alma DeGraw, she started having Thanksgiving there. The same relatives attended. Later we started going to Grandma DeBoer's. It was definitely a time to embrace family. We were always home on Christmas Eve. Dad would read Luke 2, and then we would open our gifts.

After the cottage was purchased in 1968, holidays shifted to that location, especially Memorial Day and July 4. In 1969 Phyllis delivered Tom, the second grandchild, on May 26 and was discharged on May 30, Memorial Day. She took him right from Greenville Hospital to the cottage for the holiday celebration.

Before the cottage, on hot days and after the cows were milked, we'd pile into the car and drive to Myers Lake to swim. It used to have a large, wooden pavilion that was rather scary to walk on. There'd be changing rooms and baskets to leave your clothes in while you swam. These "rooms" would be right out over the water with only a board between you and the water, which you could clearly see through all the cracks and knotholes. When you were finished you'd claim your basket by showing your number on a safety pin, dress and go home.

Later the pavilion was torn down and a beautiful beach appeared. It was close, five miles, and clean. Once it was fixed up, it started attracting a lot of people from farther away, and it became less and less appealing to us. But whether at Meyers Lake or Lincoln Lake, Dad taught us and then his grandkids how to swim. It was important to him that everyone learn.

Because of the cows and family finances, at the beginning of farming family vacations were few and far between. Ron and Phyllis remember spending a couple of days as a family in a small cabin at Olin Lakes west of Cedar Springs. It had a large pavilion and areas of the lake were sectioned off with galvanized pipes according to depth. They also remember a trip to the Upper Peninsula for a day or two and seeing Indians. Once we even took three days and drove around Lake Michigan.

The one and only trip that the six family members took together was in 1964 when we drove Ron back to his Air Force base in Tucson, AZ. We drove Route 66 round trip and were gone eight days. Our car was a brown '65 Dodge Coronet. Dad and Mother and Chuck rode in the front and Phyllis, Ron and Dar were in the back. There was never a moment of silence. If someone quit talking, Dar would sing. Mostly she sang, "Cackle . . . cackle . . . cackle," over and over again. Ron often joined her in singing.

One time, as we were driving along, everyone was getting grumpy and out of sorts. We were arguing about every little thing. Dad pulled off the road . . .and into a restaurant. And you know what, we were all in better moods once we got back into the car. After that we stopped regularly for meals. Some of our memories are of stopping in White Sands, NM and playing on the large dunes of white sand. (Whiter than even Lake Michigan sand, but probably filled with radio activity as that's where they had tested the bomb. We didn't think about such things at that time.)

We drove up Mt. Lemon in Arizona. When we'd stop at scenic lookouts, Dad would never let Dar stand on the side of the car near the drop off. He was afraid that she'd fall over because of all her liveliness. When we stopped for gas on the trip, he would make Dar run around the car ten times to calm her down. (This was the person who sang, Cackle . . .Cackle!)

We also spent a night in Roswell, NM. If we had known then what we know now, we might have stayed up all night looking for Extraterrestrials. From Tuscan we drove into Mexico. What fun and what bargains. Everyone was having a great time except Ron; he seemed rather subdued. Upon returning to Tucson we learned that service men weren't supposed to go into Mexico.

The contrast between the 50's and 60's was exemplified by what the family did for entertainment. As our affluence changed, the family began to venture further and further away from the farm. We also started to eat out more often; our first McDonald's opened on Plainfield Ave. in 1960. Dad and Mother along with Chuck and Dar made trips to Florida and to Colombia, South America. One's position in the family brings advantages and disadvantages, and travel is one of the times when it was an asset to be the younger ones.

Our favorite tree to climb, '51 or '52

Ron and Phyllis at Olin Lakes, 1952

We call this, "The Porters making
jackasses out of themselves in Mexico."
Christmas '64 when we drove Ron back to
his Air Force Base in Tuscan.

**Mother's favorite flowers, hollyhocks,
from which we girls liked to make
flower ladies**

Chapter 11

Crisis Without 911

If adversity shapes a person, then it easy to understand how our family developed into the people we are today. From Phyllis's polio, to the farmhouse burning (Chapter Two), to Dad's heart attack, to Ron's loss of a hand, we have been survivors. We never labeled these events as tragedies, disasters, or hardships. We adapted to our new circumstances, we persisted, and we conquered.

These were times that we clung to our faith. These were times that increased our faith. These were times that our friends and family closed ranks around us, protected us and encouraged us. Handling our times of crisis validated the kind of people we had hoped we were becoming.

Polio befell the family before they were farmers. Phyllis contracted it in 1944. (Chapter Two) But a pivotal decision coincided with the onset of full-time farming. Darcy and Eleanor went to see the Sister Kinney movie. It illustrated a new method of treating polio patients. It advocated muscle massage to reactivate the lost muscles rather than the bracing that took over for the muscles and caused them to atrophy. About this same time, Dr. Louis Dobbin opened his chiropractic office in Rockford. He said he would work with Phyllis if they'd take her leg brace off. This was a weighty but consequential decision to make. They knew that after having to carry her everywhere for two years, her leg brace had allowed her to finally walk on her own. Yet future years without having to wear the leg brace sounded good too. In 1947 they made the decision to take the brace off.

Eleanor took Phyllis to Dr. Dobben for therapy on her leg three times a week for two years and then two times a week for four years. Surely the income of a new farmer was stretched to provide this treatment, but it was rewarded. To this day she still walks without a leg brace. They always had to buy two pair of shoes because her feet had a difference of three shoe sizes; the shoes required extra construction in the inside also.

The summer between her 9th and 10th grades she had corrective surgery on her foot. Dr. Caulkins, a partner of the doctor who originally told Eleanor to take her daughter home, that she had only bumped her leg, reshaped her foot with a procedure called a triple orthodesis. There have been five other surgeries on her foot since that time. Buying two pair of shoes never changed, but she was finally able to wear shoes other than the orthopedic ones.

Throughout this time the family never treated Phyllis any differently. She had chores to do like any other farm girl. Her polio never held her back; the survivor mentality set in. Phyllis met her future husband while teaching at North Muskegon High School. She wondered if there would be any negative reactions from Ron toward her physical problem. Imagine her surprise to learn that his sister, Lois, had polio when she was six; Lois is a quadriplegic.

In the late 60's, through the NOSE (National Odd Shoe Exchange), Phyllis began exchanging shoes with a gal in Minnesota whose feet are the exact opposite of hers! Although they have never met, this continues to this day.

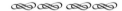

Going to the Kent County 4-H Fair was one of the highlights for us kids. When we reached the age of ten, we'd get to stay overnight at the Fair. We'd sleep in tents on cots. There would be a big one for the boys and one for the girls, or some went as families. Chuck stayed with Ingraham's. Supposedly we did this so we could "take care" of our animals, but it was also a BIG TIME for us to be at a carnival during the evening hours! Our mothers would take turns staying with us and cooking for us.

The summer of 1956, Dad and Mother had just returned home from taking Phyllis and Ron to the Kent County 4-H Fair in Lowell. They had left us with promises of being back the next day to see us show our cattle, when suddenly Dad had bad chest pains. He asked Mother to pound his back, perhaps thinking it was indigestion. He went out to do the chores, but ended up crawling on his hands and knees back to the house. Scared, Mother jumped in the car and went to get Ron from the fair.

Finally Dad allowed her to call Dr. Marco Hansen, our family doctor in Greenville. She took him to the Greenville Hospital where he stayed for three weeks. The diagnosis: a heart attack. Dad was only 39 years old. (It's interesting to note that already the concept of stress had been discovered and published by Dr. Selye.)

Phyllis remembers going to see him in the hospital for the first time. He lay in the bed with white sheets, surrounded by white walls; his face seemed so pale, and his eyes were closed. She started to cry as she thought he was dead. Just then he opened his eyes and told her he was OK. What a relief! In her hand she carried her ribbons that she had won at the Fair.

Everyone had been so kind in helping her get her cow ready to show. Everyone had wished her luck as she entered the ring. Everyone cheered when she and Emily placed first in their category of Holstein senior yearling. And everyone cheered when she and Emily re-entered the ring with the first place winners of every age category for Holsteins. And then the unthinkable happened—her Emily was designated the Grand Champion Holstein for the Kent County 4-H Fair. Her Emily, which she and her dad had bought together at an auction . . . and her dad wasn't there to join in the celebration. It all hit her as she saw her father lying so lifeless in the hospital bed. What a heart gap there is in a girl's life when her father misses those important events.

Once Dad returned home, the severity of his attack became more than real. The doctor told him to change his lifestyle. He couldn't do any heavy work. Fortunately, Walter Eckley, our Uncle Gaylord's brother-in-law, came and lived with us and did all the chores. He planted the wheat crop and harvested the corn.

This heart attack gave Dad a wake-up call, and he changed his eating and exercising habits. He used to be a big man weighing 200+ pounds; he dropped to 170. He began to take a nap each noon, and he started to exercise. Dad had been active in many organizations, and he cut back his involvement with several of them.

As a family, we were so fortunate that the heart attack turned out to be only a warning and not fatal. Father knew he had been given a second chance at life and followed this new regiment religiously.

1970 is a year that is so memorable to Ron, and to our family, that he numbers the passing years as anniversaries. It was October 19, and Ron had the self-propelled combine at some rented farm land. He was in the process of cleaning it out when he slipped and fell. His left hand got caught in the auger. Art Cavanaugh was working in his own yard nearby. As Art recounts, for some reason that he doesn't know why, he shut off the elevator that he had been using to unload corn. At that exact moment in time, he heard Ron screaming. He told Mother that at first he thought he was hearing one of the neighbor's peacocks. He found Ron walking down the road toward him.

Art immediately put Ron in his pick-up, and they headed for the Greenville Hospital. It was a foggy day, and when they came to M-57 and Evans Road, they found a unit from the State Police conducting a safety check. They stopped and asked for an escort to Greenville because of the fog. Unfortunately, they were turned away. They continued on to the hospital where Dr. Bruce Olsen did minimal first aid, covered the wound with a bandage, and gave Ron a shot of morphine.

Across the parking lot, Phyllis had just been to see Dr. Olsen at his office. He had told her that after she was dressed, she needed to go over to the hospital and get her brother, and he immediately left for the hospital. Having no clue about what had happened, she followed his instructions.

She was shocked to find Ron holding his arm upright and a bandage where his hand should have been. Dr. Olsen instructed her to take Ron to St. Mary's Hospital in Grand Rapids. She immediately asked, "Why?"

"Because they have the best hand surgeon there," replied Dr. Olsen.

At once Phyllis went to the phone and called Dad; she asked him to meet her and Ron at Wooster's Corner. (This was another wonder of timing: Dad was in the barn to take the call.) Mother had answered the phone and called him, but she listened in to the conversation.

Phyllis and Ron got into her 1963 Corvair. Ron asked her if she couldn't possibly drive any faster, but she already had the pedal to the floor. 50 to 55 *was* its top speed. Sure enough, Dad was waiting for them at Wooster's Corner. They all got into his car, which thankfully could go faster, and drove to St. Mary's Emergency.

Mother took Fred and Tom, whom she had been babysitting for Phyllis, to a friend's house and immediately went to St. Mary's in an old pickup; soon after Aunt Zelma and Pastor Adams arrived. The permission paper to amputate the rest of the hand was carefully presented for everyone to see. Dad kept reminding us that this had also happened to his grandpa, and he had been a better man because of it. Ron went into surgery just about positive that when he came out he'd be without his left hand. He was 24 years old.

That evening after returning from the hospital, the family, Tom Hough, who was living with them that year, and some neighbors gathered around the kitchen table. Dad led everyone in prayer for Ron, and through tears expressed that he wished it had been him. Darcia was so upset to see Dad cry that she went into the living room to cry herself. Tom followed and told her to stop as they all needed to be tough for Ron. Neighbors called and brought in food. Chuck set a record driving home from Michigan State University, and he went straight to the hospital. He stayed home that whole week.

Ron spent five long days in the hospital. Not only did he have to deal with the excruciating pain of the hand surgery, but the all-consuming thoughts of facing life without his left hand. Each day brought new reminders of how useful that second hand had been.

Those were the days that smoking was allowed in the hospital, and Mother, who didn't like to see Ron smoke, sat beside his bed and lit his cigarettes for him. (Smoking was allowed in hospitals until the mid 80s.) Ron had lots of friends come to visit him and to encourage him in the hospital.

The day that Ron was released from the hospital, Mother went to get him, but Ron drove the car home. They went straight to 12 Mile Road where Dad and Chuck were picking corn. Ron immediately jumped out and held up the wagon tongue to help hook up. Later that day Ron hauled corn, but he paid for it that night with pain.

At times Ron would sit on the steps going to the basement because of his pain. The torment continued a long time because he had to wrap his arm tightly with an elastic bandage to shrink the stub so he could be fitted with a prosthesis. So not only was there pain from surgery, but pain to be endured to make the arm useful again. In addition, he suffered phantom pain where his hand had been.

After three months Ron was fitted with a prosthesis. This seemed to be important to all of us. We wanted Ron to fit back into the crowd. He ended up ordering two. One was a closed hand. He wore it only two times, once for Bob Sowerby's wedding. The pinch-hook was by far the most practical and useful. He operates it by moving his shoulder. At times he would joke and tell us how it handy it was—like holding something that he was welding. Cold weather is especially hard on that arm. Ron continues to do the work of two men. To the rest of us, he almost makes it look easy. We have never heard him complain.

Tom Hough remembers, "Ron showed unequaled determination and drive to overcome his new limitation. Without complaining of the pain, he faithfully took up his new exercises to condition his stump for the prosthesis, meeting this challenge head on. He knew he could overcome the problem and did. If I remember correctly, he even showed us he could water ski with his 'hook' the next summer."

At the time of the accident, the only grandchildren were Fred and Tom, and Uncle Ron was one of their favorite people. Typical of their age, they wanted to know where Uncle Ron's hand was. We told them that Uncle Ron's hand was in heaven waiting for him—an answer that satisfied all of us.

Perhaps these stories provide some insight into the fact that most of our family has a Type A personality. We've seen examples all our lives of survivors, not quitters. We've seen family members turn unfortunate situations into workable conditions. Not once did we hear complaints about the circumstances that befell the family, and especially not from the individuals themselves.

Mother and Dad before his heart attack

Ron

Phyllis

Epilogue

The dairy cows were sold in 1971, and the dairy farm became a beef and crop farm. This continued until 1984 when Dad and Mother sold the farm on Peterson Road and had an auction sale. They moved to 11 Mile Road to a house with ten acres that backed up to Little Brower Lake. Dad continued as Township Supervisor until 1988, completing 27 years of service to Courtland Township, 15 years as Trustee and 12 years as Supervisor. He also was one of the founders of the Harvard Fire Department.

After his retirement from public office, Dad continued to serve the community by delivering hot noonday meals to the elderly and disabled for the Rockford Community Service Center. He also assisted senior citizens in the completion of Homestead Property Tax forms.

December 20, 1990, Dad and Mother celebrated their 50th anniversary. Dad had been battling cancer and passed away the next month. His positive spirit never left him even as he faced death. Dad prayed for us kids, and he and Mother talked about whom he would see in heaven.

Dad's funeral honored him as a man of faith, a successful farmer, and township servant. The service was officiated by Rev.

Jack Hough and Rev. Charles Hufstetlar, two missionaries he and Mother had supported for years. Tributes came from every corner of our community, and it was only fitting that his funeral procession of more than a mile long made its way past the farm on Peterson Road on its way to Courtland Cemetery.

Family Updates

Mother married Harold Grifhorst and spends six months in Florida and six months at Lincoln Lake in Michigan. She enjoys buying and selling antiques, and at the age of 78 got her first computer and regularly e-mails her family and friends.

Phyllis and her husband Ron Dolislager live in Tennessee. She is an author and writing consultant. They have two sons, Fredric and Thomas and four grandchildren.

Ron and his wife Beverly live in Oakfield Township. He farms 1400 acres and also buys and sells vintage John Deere tractors. They have three sons, Eric, Darcy and Bryan and four grandchildren.

Chuck and his wife Gayla live in Courtland Township. They have three children, Andrew, Kelley and Susan and five grandchildren. He farms 2400 acres in Courtland and Coral with his son, Andy. Chuck has been a part of Courtland Township administration for twelve years, four as Supervisor. As Chuck emulated Dad, Andy is also following his dad, continuing the Porter work ethic and love for farming.

Darcia and her husband Brad Kelley live in Oakfield Township. She's an educator and district director of operations. She has three children, Dennis, Danelle and Pamela and seven grandchildren.

Farm Update

The original Porter homestead on Peterson Road has succumbed to land developers. Several large homes have been constructed on the property. It makes us sad to see this "progress" taking place.

Appendix

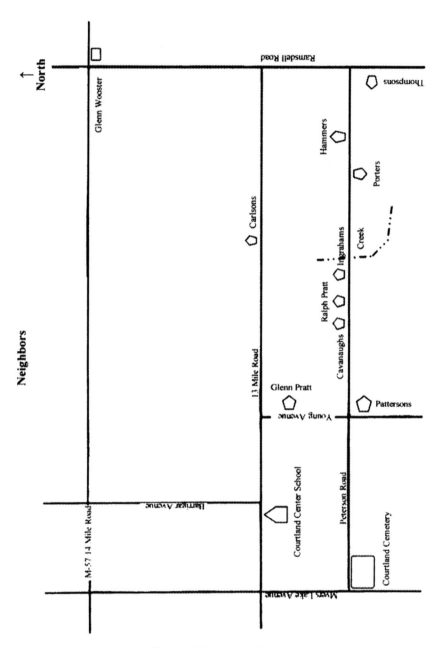

Map of Peterson Road

Porterisms

Beauty to a farmer:
 Smell of new-mowed hay
 Finish baling a field of hay and getting it all in the barn
 Fresh, plowed ground
 Field of corn
 Last load of corn picked in the fall
 Barn filled with hay
 No weeds in the field of corn
 Cows sleeping under the shade of our large Maple trees
 A dog corralling cattle

Words we hated to hear:
 The cows are out!
 It's starting to rain! *and we'd have hay on the ground*
 The water tank is overflowing!
 Milk inspector is here!
 When we needed rain, No rain again today in the weather
 forecast
 Someone is using the (phone) line . . . she's still talking.
 The bottom has gone out of Ramsdell Road. (mud-filled)
 Percy is gone!
 Dad's broken down!
 There's a tornado/funnel cloud!
 The wagon tipped over!

Way to tell how you compared with other farmers:
 Number of acres of corn and hay
 First to plant corn
 First to put up hay
 First to start harvesting
 Number of cows in the top third of the milk sheet
 How good/high your field of corn compared to others
 How straight your rows of corn were planted

Atypical things done on our farm:
Clocks were set ten minutes ahead
Have to stop work at noon for lunch—never later
Have to stop fieldwork to milk at 4:00 pm
Had to wash the car every weekend
Dad would bring Mother wild flowers.
Dad liked to dress well—thought blue chambray shirts made
    him look like an old farmer
Ground not too wet in spring to start fieldwork *until you get*
    stuck!
Hay dry enough to bale—just loosen tension so doesn't sheer pins
Mother loved hollyhocks until Dad killed them with the atrazene
We never worked on Sunday.

Mother's Sayings
Like Carter has liver pills
Hokey Pokey
I need that like I need a hole in the head
When Tozer was a pup
That's the Gospel Truth
I'll tell the world
What will the neighbors think?
You can't play, 'should have'
Don't look a gift horse in the mouth
Darn it all the heck!
Jumping up Jerusalem
I'm just not as good as you think
Dear me suds

Dad's Sayings
Hold 'er Newt
Playing cards: *Read 'em and weep*
Good Heavens
When playing Rook, *Grandma says, always feed the kitty.*
I got what Patty shot at
Today you can hear the corn grow.
It's the best thing agoin'.

Memories of Grandchildren

Fred Dolislager

I remember staying at the farm was the most exciting thing for me. Perhaps waking up on the farm was the best part. From a very early age I learned from my Uncles that I was a "city boy." What a city boy had to learn was lots of fun. You had to learn how to get up at 4:30 a.m. without an alarm clock. You had to learn how to eat!!! Grandma would provide a glass of juice and milk. In addition, would be a plate full of flapjacks, bacon, sausage, rolls, oatmeal, and cereal. I was expected to eat it all. I never could. Grandma took it personally. At times I thought she might cry because she thought I didn't like it; I was just too stuffed.

The beds at the farm were the warmest beds I ever slept in. There must have been eight inches of covers in the winter, not to mention the electric blanket. The weight of the covers would press you into the mattress. The mattresses were perhaps the softest ever. Once you were tucked in, it was impossible to roll over.

I remember Grandpa teaching me to play rook, teaching me to drive, teaching me to swim, teaching me to work, and beginning each prayer with, "Father, we bow in thy presence again and again." He was a great man in his work and in his service. I remember his fingers were as big as hotdogs. He wasn't that tall, but he had huge hands.

My special memory is the day he unintentionally broke my heart. It was then I knew how much I loved him. The story goes . . . My uncles and Grandpa were dealing with a herd of cattle that was out of control. They were trying to get them back in the barn-yard. Jackie, the dog who wasn't afraid of cows, had the cows all spooked, and they wouldn't budge while she was near. I was told to take Jackie up to the house so they could herd the cows.

Well, the herding wasn't going well, to say the least. I wanted to watch, so I took Jackie as far as the old gas pump. I stood there with Jackie sitting beside me for a while. I watched my uncles twisting the cow tails in knots to try and get them to move. Little progress was made, and little attention paid to me. Suddenly with obvious frustration in his voice, Grandpa hollered, "Fred, I said to get the dog out of here!"

Well, this was the first time I ever disappointed him. I was crushed. The dog and I ran to the house. I cried so hard into Grandma's arms that all I could say was, "Grandpa yelled at me." I can't remember if she made him come right then, or if they got the cows put up first, but Grandpa apologized. My faith in the legend of perfect grandparents was restored. My admiration of the man who could do no wrong had resumed. As other grandkids appeared on the scene (10? others) I never felt he loved me any less or any of the others any less than he loved me. He had a great capacity for showing love.

Grandma was amazing. I remember begging her to call for Grandpa just to hear the dog howl. She would holler, "Darcyyyyyy!" repeatedly. It would unnerve the dog so much that Jackie would just howl! It was great.

I remember Grandma is entirely afraid of anything reptilian or amphibian. Or mice for that matter. I remember her actually standing on a chair hollering at my uncles as they chased a mouse through the cottage. I only ever saw that on TV cartoons. What a riot! I remember the Trufant sales where Grandma taught the original "Art of the Deal."

I remember that every letter I ever received from her while in college had a little cash in it. I remembered that the more I wrote her, the more letters I got. If I had a hot date planned for a Saturday, I could write a letter on the previous Monday or Tuesday and have enough gas money by Saturday!

But the thing I remember most was Grandma's great ability to cry. Later I would catch on that this was just a statement of Grandma's great capacity for showing love. I think the first time I ever made Grandma cry was when I was prompted to belch at the breakfast table by one of my Uncles. Oh, what a disaster! Uncle laughed, I laughed at my uncle, and Grandma cried louder and louder to keep up with us. From then on, when just the right moment presented itself, it would come time to make Grandma cry!

After Grandpa died, I rode with her in the limo; then it was time to cry with Grandma.

Tom Dolislager

I remember the incredible sinking bed in the small room at the top of the stairs. You could sink a good eight inches into that mattress. Getting out was pretty difficult. I also remember that there were more blankets—and even an electric blanket—on those beds than I have experienced anywhere else.

Breakfast was an absolute treat as Grandma never failed to deliver pancakes or homemade cinnamon buns. Grandpa would always come in from work while it was still dark, and we would eat. Of course, he always caught a nap after lunch. To this day, I envy him that nap. No wonder he could stay up to watch the 11 p.m. news and still be up before dawn!

I will never forget the ceramic, black-stove, cookie jar that always seemed to be full of Wrigley's gum. We could take whatever we wanted and didn't even have to ask. That seemed like sheer decadence.

I remember Grandma's baking. There was none better, and it just kept coming: bread, cinnamon rolls, pancakes, huckleberry pies, blueberry pies, apple pies. As far as cooking went, Grandma had a signature, if not ubiquitous, meal: Meat and Potatoes. I loved it then and love it still.

I loved going to the flea market with Grandma as she looked for hidden treasures and sold her wares. I was proud of her savvy. She just did not make bad deals.

When I would drive up from Wheaton College for a visit, Grandpa would always gas up the old Mustang and have the oil changed. Somehow he managed to get this done before I even woke up. Often I would not even notice until after I had left. He didn't even want recognition. He just wanted to help. What generosity.

I loved going to the spa with Grandpa. He would lift weights and swim with me. As I began serious lifting for high school sports, he would proudly spot me as I lifted and brag to all of his cronies that I was his grandson. We always stopped by the bakery on the way back for some donuts. I love the way Grandpa would perpetually take one-half of a donut or sweet roll. I don't think I ever saw him eat a whole one—in one sitting.

Andy Porter

Grandson Nights: I remember doing push-ups and sit-ups with Grandpa and watching cartoons on Saturday mornings. They also took us to the Shrine Circus.

The first dollar I ever made was helping Grandpa do hay when I was about five years old. He gave me a brand new dollar bill at the end of the day. He also took me to the candy store with the boat at Lincoln Lake.

Once I was with Grandma in the Ford LTD on the way home from Mc Donald's, and she had a "fender bender." I also remember all the plates she collected and hung on the walls.

Susan Porter Meek

I remember when all the girls and Grandma went for a walk around the lake. It was snowing, and Grandma got stuck in a snow bank. We all had to help get her out.

Danelle and I were Grandpa's two twins. Grandpa used to dress up as Santa Claus at Christmas. One time he got us to memorize John 3:16. Grandma used to crush aspirin in a spoon and feed it to us if we weren't feeling well.

Danelle Nauta

Granddaughter Nights: I remember doing twenty sit-ups, jumping jacks and push-ups in the morning with Grandpa. I remember ice-skating on Little Brower Lake, and I remember going to North Kent Mall with the whole dollar Grandpa used to give us girls.

My special memory of Grandpa is the day I found out he had cancer. I remember crying while <u>he</u> hugged <u>me</u>, and I remember thinking how strong and brave he was. My special memories of Grandma are the many hours she put in working with me on the Spelling Bee and actually traveling down to Indianapolis with me one year.

Pam Nauta

Granddaughter Nights: I remember exercises in the morning, ice-skating on Brower Lake, and walking around Brower Lake and getting stuck in the snow. Grandpa would lead us in exercises every morning.

I remember Grandpa's big, but gentle, hands. He was the best Rook player around. I only remember seeing him upset once. One day we threw small rocks in the bottom of the swimming pool to dive in and find. That was the first time Grandpa scolded us, and I remember feeling so bad that I'd let him down.

Special memories of Grandma include SUGAR PILLS. Even if we weren't sick, we would want one! Also bears, plates, antiques, and Trufant. She always gave us a dollar to spend on Granddaughter Nights. She played the organ for the family to sing Christmas carols, and she was always humming! I loved her crazy jewelry—especially her earrings. Her favorite color was purple. She has tiny hands.

We loved getting Grandma to laugh about everything. She would laugh so hard she would cry. Everyone always tried to get her to cry! It was very easy. Grandma gave me my first perm and cut all of my hair off to make me look like a boy. She was the best baker around, and you could never leave her house without eating something.

Grandpa and Grandma loved each other so much—it was obvious to everyone. They were the best example to live by as husband and wife, father and mother, grandpa and grandma. I just hope that someday my kids will know their Great Grandma and experience the love I was given as a child and now as an adult. I feel deeply privileged to have had the world's best grandparents, and I hope they will know how much of an impact they have made.

**Tom and Fred arriving for a visit
to the farm**

**Tom and Fred wearing their
"barn boots"**

Fred and Dad playing Rook

Dad playing Santa for the grandchildren

Darcy, named after Dad, Ron and Dad

**Pam, Kelly, Danelle, and Susan exercising with
Grandpa**

Grandpa leading grandsons in push-ups

Grandpa leading Darcy and Brian in jumping jacks

**Granddaughter Night with Susan, Danelle,
Grandma, Kelly and Pam with Grandma**

**Dad and Mother with all their
grandchildren, 1987**

Grand Rapids Press

January 1, 1949

Uncle Wiggily's New Year

Several times on the afternoon that Mr. Whitewash brought home Bunty and Buster in the little bark toy shop, Uncle Wiggily blew his big horn. He was celebrating the going away of the old year of 1948 and the coming of the New Year of 1949.

"Wiggy! Wiggy! Why do you make so much noise?" asked his wife.

"Because I am happy, my dear," answered the rabbit gentleman. "Does the blowing of my New Year horn bother you?"

"Well, it makes Nurse Jane jump every time you toot it," said the rabbit lady.

"Jumping is good for Nurse Jane," said Uncle Wiggily.

"It isn't when she has eggs in her paws," said Mrs. Longears. She was looking out of the door to the lawn in front of her hollow stump bungalow where Uncle Wiggily stood blowing his big horn.

"Why isn't it good for Nurse Jane to jump when she has eggs in her paws, my dear?" Uncle Wiggily looked at his wife. "Why isn't it?"

"Because, Wiggy, every time you toot your horn and Nurse Jane jumps, she drops an egg on the kitchen floor. She has dropped three so far and the floor is quite mess."

"Oh, I'm sorry about that," said Uncle Wiggily, "I'll stop blowing my horn. But what is Nurse Jane doing with so many eggs?"

"She is making a pudding for our New Year's day dinner," answered Mrs. Longears. "And if she drops any more eggs, you'll have to go to the store for some. And the store may be closed on account of this being New Year's day, and then you'll have to go to the coop of Mrs. Cluck Cluck, the hen lady, to get eggs. So you'd better stop blowing your horn."

"I better had, I guess," said Uncle Wiggily twinkling his nose. His nose was pink, as you may remember.

The rabbit gentleman put his horn back in his bungalow. He was wondering what he might do to have an adventure this first day of the New Year when he heard Bunty calling:

"Uncle Wiggily! Uncle Wiggily!"

"Yes, Bunty! What is it?"

"Please come and see the new play house that Mr. Whitewash

189

set up for us in the back yard. It's wonderful!"

"Yes, I'll come and look at it," said Uncle Wiggily.

He found Bunty and some of the little rabbit girls playing in the make-believe bark toy shop that Eenie the wolverine had set up in the woods as a trap to catch little rabbits.

Mr. Whitewash had rescued Buster and Bunty from the wolverine and Bobbie the bobcat. The Polar bear had brought the bark house home to Uncle Wiggily's bungalow. It was just right for little rabbits.

"Isn't it lovely?" asked Bunty.

"It certainly is," said the rabbit gentleman. "Mr. Whitewash told me there was a toy canoe and doll in this bark house when you and Buster found it."

"That's right, Uncle Wiggily. Mr. Whitewash took those toys to Totty a little puppy dog and his sister. Santa Claus sort of forgot them."

"Well, then I guess everyone is happy this New Year's day. I know I am." said Uncle Wiggily. And he was happier when Nurse Jane called him into the bungalow to help eat the egg pudding.

That night Uncle Wiggily was suddenly awakened by hearing a noise near the new playhouse. Looking out of the window, the rabbit gentleman saw the wolverine sneaking over the snow.

"Ho! Ho! He has come back to get his bark house," said Uncle Wiggily. "I'll make him run!" the gentleman blew on his horn three loud blasts: Toot! Toot! Toot! Away ran Eenie the wolverine and Bunty still had her new play house.

So if the apple pie doesn't have to jump out of the bread box to look for its piece of cheese, I'll tell you another story on Monday.

Courtland Clippings From 1965

The Rockford Register
January 14, 1965

Courtland Clippings

Mrs. Darcy Porter

———————————

Many thanks to Elizabeth Keech for taking over the column while I was gone. We are glad to be back in Michigan but had a good trip. We saw cotton being picked and visited a cotton gin, visited White Sands Missile Base in New Mexico and also went to Old Mexico for a day. Our son Ron drove us on a tour of Mt. Lemmon by Tucson, which was 25 miles up. Skiing was being enjoyed on the top. The children went swimming New Years Day. Visited the air base where Ron is stationed.

The Courtland WSCS will sponsor Miss Mildred Drescher on January 21 at 2:00 at the church. She will review the book "The Nation and the Kingdom." All women of the charge are cordially invited to attend.

Harriette and Roberta Keech had the 4th knitting club meeting at their home Saturday. This coming Saturday, Barbara and Linda White will be the hostesses.

Sunday dinner guests of the Aaron Porters were Mr. and Mrs. Mel Nelson and boys of Lowell.

We wish to extend our sympathy to Mrs. Dale Dines in the loss of her mother this week, Mrs. Mary Northrup of Sand Lake.

Alice and Ralph Pratt attended the Michigan Milk Leaders Conference at Kellogg Center last week Monday and Tuesday.

Next Monday Courtland Extension meeting will be at my home at 8 p.m. The lesson will be on "Influence of a Changing Society on American Marriage." Bertha Norman will be the leader.

New Years Day Rose and Forrest Gould called on Mary and Harry Connant.

Saturday Mrs. Nina Hardy of Rockford and Rose Gould called on the Carl Smith family in Kalamazoo.

Listen for the wedding bells this week in the community.

Sunday callers at the John DeBoer home were Mr. and Mrs. Charles Johnson, Mrs. Wilma Visser, Mr. and Mrs. Ben Den Braber of Grand Rapids, Mr. and Mrs. Clare Souffrou of Belmont and Mr. and Mrs. Dan Johnson.

Saturday night Aaron and Dedee Porter attended the travelogue at the Civic on Hawaii. They were guests later of her parents, the John Derteins of Jenison.

Saturday Alice Pratt, Linda Rogers and Ann Scott, Caroline Pratt and Lola Carlson attended a shower at Mrs. Clark Carlson's home in honor of Mary Fessenden who will become the bride of Steven Carlson this Saturday.

Thursday night the Stinson Booster Club meeting will be held at 8:00. Let's have a good turnout.

Mr. and Mrs. George Keech and girls and Mrs. Charles Keech enjoyed Sunday dinner out at the Country Kitchen at Laingston.

Darcia Porter celebrated her eleventh birthday Thurs. Sharon Porter and Lois Botts were her supper guests.

Ann and Jim Scott and Timmy were Saturday supper guests at the Ralph Pratt home.

Mr. and Mrs. Forrest Gould were Sunday dinner guests at Ralph and Maxine Goulds.

Wayne and Anna Whittall called on hospital patients Saturday night. Roy Whittall at Blodgett and Lloyd Brownell and wife Verne who are both patients at Butterworth. Lloyd's room is 524 and Verne's 625. We wish them all a speedy recovery.

Mrs. Joe Eltsner and son Alfred of Martinsville, Ind. former Algoma residents were Saturday overnight guests of Walter and Mary Carpenter. Saturday evening Mary Carpenter and Mrs. Elstner called on Mrs. Frank Hockeborn.

There will be a card party at the grange this Saturday the 16th.

Carroll and Betty Patterson were Saturday night guests of Kay and George Wilsted. Wednesday the Wilsteds were guests of the Pattersons.

Mrs. Frank Hockeborn was a Sunday dinner guests at the Robert Norman home.

Well child Clinic will be open only once a month this winter. It will meet the first Wednesday of every month at Oakfield Baptist Church.

Leone Post is our new Avon representative for this area.

Sunday Mrs. Helen Williams, Mrs. Ethel Williams, Mr. and Mrs. Harold Williams and Mr. and Mrs. Alvin Ingraham attended the funeral of their nephew and cousin, Bruce Williams of Reed City who met accidental death this past week. He was a young man of 34 and left five children besides his wife. We extend our sympathy.

Sunday, Mr. and Mrs. Carroll Patterson and family called on Mr.

and Mrs. Arthur Taylor and family of Grand Rapids.

Thursday was June Ingraham's birthday. Callers in the evening to wish her a happy birthday were Mrs. Helen Williams and Mrs. Ethel Williams and family.

Mr. and Mrs. Gene Post and family were Sunday night guests of Dick and Arlene Cole of Bostwick Lake. Everyone enjoyed watching the football game on color TV.

The Rockford Register
January 21, 1965

Courtland Clippings

Mrs. Darcy Porter

Courtland Center Community Club will be February 4, (Thursday). Tad Risius, exchange student from Germany will be speaking and showing pictures.

Gene and Leone Post attended a Progressive Supper Saturday held by the couples club of the Bostwick Lake Church. Wesley and Phyllis Hessler also were one of the couples. They all report a good time despite the cold weather.

Kenneth and Irma Becker and Gary called on her brother and family, Mr. and Mrs. James Roberts of Coral Sunday afternoon.

Leone Clement drove Terry last Monday to his rabbit club meeting by Ada. The club meets once a month.

Mrs. Emerson Clement received word her cousin, Glen Ruck of Lansing, passed away Sunday. He was brought to Greenville for burial. We extend our sympathy.

Chuck Porter was a Friday overnight and Saturday guest of Gordon Pratt to help him celebrate his birthday. Gordon will celebrate his 13th birthday Thursday.

Congratulations to the newly-weds, Mr. and Mrs. Steven Carlson who were married Saturday evening at the Courtland Methodist Church. Mrs. Carlson is the former Mary Fessenden.

Linda Post celebrated her 10th birthday last week. We wish her a happy birthday too.

While we are on the subject of birthdays, we also wish Kim White one, he was 11 last Friday. Eddie Norton was a guest for cake and ice cream.

Ron Porter will celebrate his 19th birthday in Tucson Wednesday of this week.

The 4-H knitting club will meet with their leader Mrs. Margaret Hale's home this Saturday.

Sunday evening guests of D.M. White and Nita after attending services at the Rockford Reformed Church were Mr. and Mrs. Max Moon and Mr. and Mrs. John Wierda.

Saturday night guests of George and Elizabeth Keech were Mr. and Mrs. Lyman Clark and son Dave of Casnovia.

Saturday evening guests of the LeRoy Brownells were Ralph and Margie Lovelace and David and Evelyn. They enjoyed seeing "The Swan" on color TV.

Mrs. Mary Brownell attended the March of Dimes meeting Thursday in Grand Rapids.

Last Thursday Theron Wheat, Glen Pratt, Forrest Squires, Darcy Porter and Max Bird attended the Annual Township Officers Meeting in Lansing at the Jack Tar Hotel.

Mrs. Blanche Hessler is in Butterworth Hospital for treatment.

Mr. and Mrs. Kenneth Becker were Sunday evening guests of the Albert Beckers of Edgerton.

We were Friday night callers at my folks, the John DeBoers, and showed them our slides we took on our trip.

Morey and Norma Beemer and girls were Sunday dinner guests of her parents Mary and Roy Brownell.

Mr. and Mrs. Tom Miller and new baby, Laura Marie are spending this week at their aunts home, Mr. and Mrs. Harold Bailey Jr. of Meyers Lake. Laura Marie was born Friday.

Mrs. Aaron Porter helped chaperone a senior young people ice skating party Saturday night. Skating was done on the Silver Jack Wannagen pond.

Sharon, Keith and Brad Wheat were Sunday dinner guests of her parents, the Forrest Squires.

Ethel Brownell is a patient in Sheldon Memorial Hospital in Albion, Mich. She is coming along nicely.

Mr. and Mrs. Gerald Stotz Sr. spent Sunday with their son and family, Mr. and Mrs. Gerald Stolz, Jr. of Royal Oak.

Mr. and Mrs. Aaron Porter and family were Sunday dinner guests of Mr. and Mrs. John Dertein of Jenison.

Mr. and Mrs. Henry Moulter and family spent Saturday with his parents, Mr. and Mrs. Otis Moulter of Howard City. Mrs. Moulter had just returned home from the Kelsey Hospital last week with a broken shoulder and arm.

Barton Ingraham spent the weekend at Western Michigan College in Kalamazoo.

Tade Risius accompanied Paul Robe, Ivan Lair and Jim Hines to Lake City where they attended a bear hunters yearly meeting.

Sunday afternoon Al and June Ingraham called on the Melvin Nielsen family at Greenville. On the way home, they stopped at Ethel Williams home to pick up Helen and Brian who had spent the day with their cousins.

Darcia Porter was a Sunday dinner and afternoon guest of Brenda Moon of Podunk.

Sunday lunch guests of Bob and Bertha Norman were her brother and family, Mr. and Mrs. Frances Hockeborn and family of Sparta.

The Rockford Register
March 25, 1965

Courtland Clippings

Mrs. Darcy Porter

Saturday night the young adults from the Courtland and Oakfield Methodist Churches will meet at George and Elizabeth Keech's home at 7:30.

There will be a card party at the Courtland Grange Saturday.

Sunday evening there will be a fellowship hour at the Oakfield Methodist Church. Tad Risius will show his slides of Germany. Be there at 7:30.

This week there is a Global Missionary Conference every night at the Rockford Baptist Church. A different missionary from many countries will speak every night.

Allen Erhart was home for the weekend with his parents, Ed and Gladys Erhart. Also, Carol is home for this week for her between terms vacation. Allen attends the U of M in Ann Arbor and Carol at Michigan State.

We wish to extend our sympathy to the Carroll Patterson family in the sudden death of Carroll's brother, Arthur Taylor.

Saturday night Carroll and Betty Patterson and Sandra and

Shirley and Tom DeYoung were at Mr. and Mrs. Robert Newkirks home in Grand Rapids to visit with Wallace Heinzelman who came from Florida to attend Arthur Taylor's funeral.

Friday night, Mrs. Aaron Porter and Mr. and Mrs. Arthur Porter attended the wedding of their cousin, Sandra Dertein to Jim Joldersma in Grand Rapids at the Redeemer Lutheran Church.

Mr. and Mrs. D.M. White and family were Friday supper guests of Mr. and Mrs. Richard Dennie of Podunk.

Mr. and Mrs. Leroy Brownell enjoyed having all their family home Sunday. Allen Brownell from Chattanooga, Tenn. and Judy Bennett of Lansing, Walter and Sue Brownell and Norma and Morey Beemer and Debbie and Barbara completed the family circle.

Mr. and Mrs. Glowen Reyburn had Sunday dinner with Mr. and Mrs. Leo Reyb urn in Muskegon, in the evening they called on their son, Mr. and Mrs. DeVerl Reyburn and family of Cedar Spring.

My parents, Mr. and Mrs. John DeBoer were Saturday night guests in our home.

Ralph and Maxine Gould and family were Saturday evening guests of Glen and Hardene Pratt and boys.

We wish Shirley Patterson a Happy Birthday. Shirley's birthday was Monday. Sunday the family enjoyed "dinner out" at the Country Kitchen at Langston.

Mr. and Mrs. Aaron Porter and family were Sunday evening lunch guests of Mr. and Mrs. Robert Peck.

Saturday, Leone and Avery Clement called on Leone's mother, Mrs. Beardslee, who is a patient at Mercy Hospital in Muskegon. While they were gone, Terry Clement had the misfortune to fall and break his nose.

Sunday Charles and Imogene Clement and Avery and Leone and boys drove by Spencer Grange to see the herd of deer that has been attracting so much attention in that vicinity. They report more than 100 in the herd.

Sunday dinner guests of Ralph and Alice Pratt were Mr. and Mrs. Harry Carlson and Arlene, Mr. and Mrs. Joe Carlson, Mr. and Mrs. Roy Dunaven, Fred Carlson, Mr. and Mrs. Clark Carlson and Edna Carlson.

The Pioneer Girls of Oakfield Baptist church will have their first Encampment Monday, March 29. Their mothers are invited to see the girls receive their badges and awards.

Mr. and Mrs. Henry Moulter and family called on Mr. and Mrs. Don Hyder and family of Brower Lake Sunday afternoon.

Mr. and Mrs. Robert Simpson had Sunday dinner in Greenville with Mr. and Mrs. Victor Sorensen.

Saturday callers of Mr. and Mrs. Glowen Reyburn were their son and family, Mr. and Mrs. Gordon Reyburn.

Al and June Ingraham and family and Tad Risius visited over the weekend with Mr. and Mrs. Philo Ingraham of Lapaz, Ind.

Monday night, the Courtland Township treated the Volunteer Firemen to a chicken dinner served by the ladies of the Courtland Grange. Men were from the Harvard and Rockford departments. Pictures were shown by Jim Squires of the Conservation department. These men deserve a big thank you for how willing they are to give their help and time when any of us have a fire.

Mr. and Mrs. Gaylord DeBoer and family enjoyed visiting the Grand Rapids Museum Sunday afternoon.

The Rockford Register
April 22, 1965

Courtland Clippings

Mrs. Darcy Porter

_____

Several relatives and friends of this area suffered loss from the tornado storm a week ago. Among some were Walter and Sue Brownell who while in their trailer home overturned three times. They were badly bruised up but glad to be alive. Their trailer was completely demolished. At present, they are with Walt's parents, Mary and Roy Brownell.

Ralph and Maxine Gould also suffered the complete loss of their new home in Edgerton. Maxine was a patient in Butterworth at the time. She came home Wednesday. Their children were at the Glen Pratts last week, and this week Maxine, Ralph and youngest are still with them while the older ones are at their aunts, Margie Gould and grandparents, the Albert Beckers.

My folks, John DeBoers, lost their barn and garage and back of their house. Also damage to Theron Wheat's barn and garage

of the Arthur Stoops. Gaylord DeBoer's had damage to their house.

Mr. Albert Burgess is in St. Mary's hospital for surgery. He would enjoy a card from you. Room 237.

Sunday dinner and evening guests of Carroll and Betty Patterson were Mr. and Mrs. Hohmer Lytle, Mrs. Pauline Petersen, and Mrs. Grace Godfrey.

Mark Bogdanik, Leonard Post and Chuck Porter are among the 7th grader campers at Chief Noonday Camp this week at Yankee Springs.

Wayne and Anna Whittall drove to Alpena Monday and visited her Mother's grave there and drove on to Gaylord for a load of seed potatoes and came home Tuesday.

Wednesday callers of the Roy Brownells were Martin Wacha and wife Beth and girls of Greenville.

Carol Erhart was home for her spring vacation from Michigan State this past week and returned to Lansing Monday.

Mr. and Mrs. Aaron Porter and family were Easter dinner guests of the John Derteins of Jenison.

Easter dinner guests of Wayne and Anna Whittall were Peg and John Goller and family and D.M. and Nita White and family.

A week ago, on the 10th, Henry and Jessie Moulter, George and Elizabeth Keech and Phyllis Hessler helped Eleanor Case celebrate her birthday at her home. They were evening lunch guests.

My folks were Sunday dinner guests at our home.

Saturday evening, the young adults from Courtland and Oakfield Methodist Church will meet at Betty and Dick Houting's home.

The annual Ham Supper of the Courtland Grange will be April 29. Serving will start at 5:30.

A week ago Wesley Hessler went to Mobile, Alabama on business.

Sunday, Avery and Leone Clement enjoyed a Sunday drive and visited Mr. and Mrs. Henry Heitz of 10 Mile Road near Sparta. In the evening, they called on Mr. and Mrs. Harold Strowbridge of Meyers Lake to see their new baby boy born the night of the storm.

Jane Hessler visited her cousin, Diane Dibble in Lansing a few days last week, while David Dibble visited with the Hesslers here. Jane's uncle flew her home in his plane Wednesday night.

Mr. and Mrs. Otis Moulter and Gilbert Moulter of Howard City spent Sunday with the Henry Moulter family.

Saturday night, Aaron and Dedee Porter had a party for Aaron's college age Sunday school class.

Tracey and Jack White and family were Easter dinner guests of Mr. and Mrs. John Oldenkamp.

Mrs. Charles Keech had Sunday dinner with A.O. and Dorothy Richardson at Brower Lake and were lunch guests of George and Elizabeth Keech.

Mr. and Mrs. Robert Simpson were Sunday supper guests of Dr. and Mrs. A.J. Gasick of Grand Rapids.

Mr. and Mrs. LeRoy Brownell had Mr. and Mrs. Frank Wacha of Belding and Walter and Sue Brownell for Easter dinner guests. Norma and Morrey Beemer and girls were evening lunch guests.

Darcy and I and Chuck and Darcia attended Good Friday services with Aaron and Dedee Porter and were lunch guests there later.

Kenneth Colby and Ken Jr. spent Saturday helping Mr. and Mrs. John DeBoer with tornado clean up.

Easter dinner guests of Ralph and Alice Pratt were Ann and Jim Scott and Timmy, Linda and Ron Rogers and Chris and Mrs. Georgia Pratt. Afternoon callers were Mr. and Mrs. Harry Carlson and

Arlene, Fred Carlson, Mrs. Roy
Dunaven, Edna Carlson, Shirley
Patterson and Mr. and Mrs. Ross
Pratt and family.

Friday evening callers of the
Roy Brownells were Viola and
William Allersma.

Phyllis Porter and Ron
Dolislager were visitors in our
home last week, also my mother
and Gary and David DeBoer for a
couple days.

Letter from Otto Krause

WOLVERINE SHOE & TANNING CORP.
Tanners and Manufacturers of Shoes and Gloves

ROCKFORD, MICH. 12/24/40

G. ADOLPH KRAUSE
PRESIDENT
VICTOR W. KRAUSE,
SECRETARY
OTTO A. KRAUSE,
TREASURER

Eleanor De Boer Porter
Rockford, Mich.

Friend Eleanor: Happiness in married life comes as it does in all our undertakings thru unselfish service. When two married people learn to forget self and act and think always in all reasonable ways and things for the happiness of the other, then and then only will they realize the life of which they dreamed.

The life you may surely find and hold the true way to your end.

Sincerely

Wolverine Shoe [Tannery?]

Otto A. Krause.

Department of Vocational Agriculture Diploma

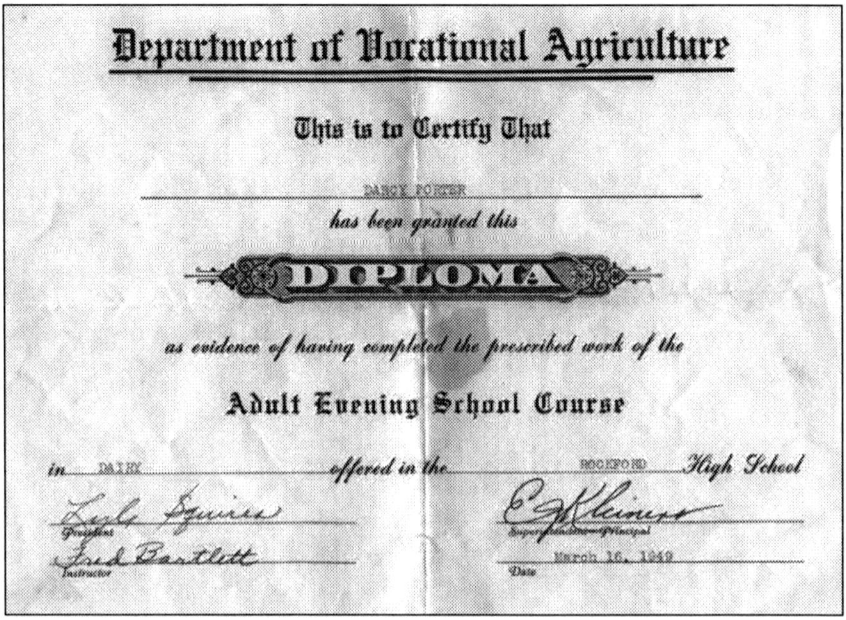
Department of Vocational Agriculture

This is to Certify That

DARCY PORTER

has been granted this

DIPLOMA

as evidence of having completed the prescribed work of the

Adult Evening School Course

in DAIRY *offered in the* ROCKFORD *High School*

President

Fred Bartlett
Instructor

Superintendent—Principal

March 16, 1949
Date

Farm Diary 1963

January

1   Phyllis & Marilyn were here for dinner and left. Uncle Ben and Aunt Tina came.

2   Kids went back to school. All went to prayer meeting.

3   1 steer 8:30 a.m.—Jack $567.03

4   Went and saw Uncle Gary to hospital and Mrs. Baker. Chuck and Dar stayed at Ma's.

5   Ron went to YFC. Chuck went to 1ᵗ Sat. basketball. Dar went to Pioneer girls.

6   Went to church. Ma and Dad and Grandma Porter came for dinner.

7   Darcia's birthday. Had 3 girls for supper after school. Darcy and Ron went to tractor meeting.

8   Lions Club dinner—Darcy. Went to Ladies Missionary. Saw Fern in the hospital. Received $166 from steer at Ada Beef Co.

9   Darcy and I drove to GR to Mich. Milk Producers for supplies. Went to prayer meeting. Got ice cream after to Buena Vista for Darcia's birthday. Ken K. brought Ron home.

10   Dairy Banquet. Sue and Ron and us went to Sparta to the banquet. Had good time. Darcy and I went to Greenville and saw Fern in the afternoon. Linda Ingraham is Dairy Queen.

11   Went to Rockford. Saw Crystal. Took Chuck for his lesson. Went to Cedar to basketball game. Lost 65 to 51.

12   Stayed home at night. It stormed so. Chuck went to Sat. basketball and Dar to Pioneer Girls.

13   Went to Sunday school and church both times in severe snowstorm. Ron had Sue to church at night. Hardly made it home when he took her home. He was the last one on our road.

14   14 in. of snow and more coming. No school. Wind 28 mph. 7:30 p.m.—3°—6 more inches by nighttime. 8:45—5°. Chuck and Ron played basketball at Hammers' for a while.

15   18° below in morning. 27° below in Cedar. No School. 15° below here. 20° below at all neighbors. Ron drove to Cedar and saw Sue too. All our cars started but Ron's. Dad (Grandpa DeBoer) got his cast off and another on.

16   2° below zero in a.m. Went to Rockford and got groceries. Saw Dad and Mrs. Leareen. Our car couldn't start. Dead battery. All went to prayer meeting. Only 29 out in all.

17   Zero today. MABC meeting at Courtland Grange—8 p.m. Darcy and I drove to Rockford. Saw his mother. Dedee came in afternoon and all the kids stayed. She came back for supper. Ron finished semester tests. 20° at 9:30 p.m.

18   Kids home from school. We all drove to Sparta and looked at tractors. We went to Reva's at night. Chuck stayed at Gordon Pratt's all night. Went to Greenville in the afternoon. Ron and Sue went to game at Rockford. Rockford 86 and Lowell 49.

19   was all day to Gordon's. Dar at Pioneer Girls. Ron and Ken went to YFC (Youth for Christ) at night. Ken's car broke. Sue's dad brought them home.

20 Ron's birthday — 17 years old. High of 11°, low of 2°. 140 in S.S. Didn't go to church at night. Very bad storm. Ma and Dad and Darcy's mother couldn't come. Sue was here for dinner.

21 7° below in a.m. No school. Our car and Ron's wouldn't start. Darcy left the lights on. Ron went to Sue's in afternoon. Back at night with Ken Kraus to get battery out of his car. Darcy went to Deacon's meeting. I went to Extension at Mrs. Simpson's.

22 Zero. All schools closed but Rockford. Darcia stayed home with a bad cough. Beacon class party postponed. Went to Mrs. Jones' funeral. Mr. Adams had it. Dedee and Aaron went with us. Phyllis came home for between semesters (at Central Michigan University). Played Rook at night.

23 Was below zero. Kids all went to school. We all went to prayer meeting at night. Ron and Phyl and Darcy and I played Rook.

24 Dairy meeting 10 a.m. to 3 pm. Took Dad to G.R. (6:50 p.m. Lions meeting at Sr. High School). Big blizzard came. School let out early. Darcy stayed home at night. We all played Rook and had pizza in the living room.

25 Little warmer today — 8° above. Phyllis went to dentist. Darcy and I drove to Greenville. Left truck for tires. Drove Carl's car home. We all went to Uncle Gary's for the evening.

26 8° above. Real nice day. Went to library. Phyllis went to circus. Rest of us stayed home at night.

27 Best Sunday in 4 weeks. 163 in S.S. Went to Pioneer Girls Encampment at Grace Bible. Darcia received 3 awards and played the offertory. We went to Dedee's and Aaron's for

lunch. Was to Ma and Dad's for dinner. Phyllis and Ron went to North Park Church.

28 4° below today. Nice otherwise. Phyllis and Darcy went to Cedar. They drove a new Falcon around. Hauled Ken K's car home. Carlton was over in afternoon. We all played Rook last night.

29 2° below in a.m. 17° high. Rector's and us went out for dinner to Country Kitchen. Went to Beacon Class Party at night. Was on Food Committee. Ron can't drive to school for a month. He drove at noon hour.

30 Kids went to school and we all went to prayer meeting. Played Rook awhile.

31 Darcy and Phyllis and I went to G.R. Got Ron's application for S.S. Number. Had dinner at G.R. Buffet Style. Got groceries. We all played Rook at night.

February

1 Went to Rockford and to Greenville. Dedee went too. Phyllis and Chuck and Ron went to B. Game. Rockford beat Sparta.

2 Nice and warm and icy. Phyllis went back in afternoon. Darcia and I went to Mayfield Christian School to a Pioneer Girls Rally. I drove a load down of women. Got home at 8:45 p.m. Darcy and the boys stayed home.

3 4° below. Cold and sunny. Went to church. Went to Grandpa DeBoer's for his birthday in afternoon. At night Bidstrups came home for lunch after church.

4 10° above and windy. Darcy and I were at Leareen's to get cow money. Went to Rockford. Saw Darcy's mother. Sent

two beef to Machoffers. Darcy went to Hugh Long's to Ag Class. The kids and I played Rook at night.

5   32° Nice and sunny out. Little thawing. Darcy and I drove south of Ionia to see some tractors and cows on a sale. Went to Ladies Missionary.

6   8:00 p.m. Forrest Squires Twp. Meeting. Went to Prayer Meeting. Emily got worse. Had Dr. Green twice today. Duane and Rita were here at night.

7   Thawing today. Had to take Emily away. Went to work meeting at Ellene's. Ron's boyfriend was here for supper. He and Ron went to party at Fuller's. Anderson's were here at night to work on church history.

8   2° below. Art and Ruth were here for supper. Ron went to the Auto Show again with boyfriends.

9   We stayed home at night and watched TV and played Rook with all the kids.

10   Young people had the service. Went to church. Ken K. came in afternoon. Ron had dinner at Rogers. Played Rook at night after church.

11   32°. Real nice. Darcy and Ron went to sale south of Ionia. I went shopping to Arlan's and Miracle Mart. Darcy went to Ag Class at Rockford with Dayton at night.

12   Real cold in morning. Went to 32°. Real nice out. Rode to Rockford and saw Crystal. Darcy bought a cow for $258 from Normans.

13   Road Commission meets at Forest S. at 10 a.m. Went to Prayer Meeting. Darcy went to Road Commission Meeting.

I went to town. Saw Mrs. Leareen and Dedee and Darcy's mother.

14   Dad and Mother and Joyce and Gaylord and Grandpa and Alma were here for dinner for Dad's birthday. Dad and Mother were here for supper. Ron went to Greenville to play basketball with Calvary Church.

15   Zero. Les. B. was here today. Dedee too. Darcy went to Rockford. I went to Greenville. Got groceries. Darcy and Chuck and Ron went to basketball game. Rockford lost to Cedar. Real close game.

16   7° below zero in morning. 1:30 p.m. caucus. Darcy went to caucus. Darcia went to Pioneer Girls and went with Dedee to the dog races in Sparta. We all played Rook at night.

17   Went to church both times. Ron was to Rectors at noon for dinner and at Krauses' at night. We were to Newmans at night. We called Phyllis in the afternoon. Chuck played piano at night.

18   Darcy went to Business Meeting at church.

19   Stayed home all day and night. Dar had Marla P. home overnight. The rest of us played Rook.

20   5° above zero, real windy. Went and got meat at Morhoffer's. Went to prayer Meeting. Homer Baker spoke. Ron brought Ken and Jody P. home.

21   4° below zero. Darcy and I went to Ma and Dad's for dinner. Ma and I went after groceries and present for Alma. At night Ken Krause and Jody were here and played Rook.

22   5° below. Real bad out. Darcy had to get pipes thawed out by welder at Zelma's. Darcia and I went to Alma and Grandpa's

for her birthday. Phyllis arrived home at 5 with Ruth. They went to Wealthy Church at night with Judy R.

23 Chuck played ball. Dar went to a party. Ice skating in afternoon. Ron went to YFC with Nancy Rogen. We played Rook and watched TV at night. Had barbecues in the living room.

24 Went to church. Phyllis and Ruth went back. We went to see Hammers in the afternoon. Went to church at night.

25 Took car to Greenville to have speedometer fixed. I went to a meeting at church and Darcy and Dayton went to an Ag Meeting at Rockford.

26 Kids went to school. We stayed home at night. Darcy didn't feel good.

27 10° below zero. Went to prayer meeting. Darcy stayed home. Didn't feel good. I went through Wolverine and Tannery. Chuck practiced for Talent Show.

28 20° today. Went to Cedar and got license for pickup. Stopped and saw Ma and Dad. Saw Grandpa and Alma. Chuck went skating with Hammers. Ron played basketball in Greenville.

March

1 2° below low, 32° high. Went to Rockford and Grand Rapids. Darcy got a razor from Ron Pace. Darcy and Ron went car shopping.

2 Chuck went to last of Sat. gym. Dar to Pioneer Girls. Ron and Sue went to YFC. We all stayed home.

3 Went to Sunday school and church. Darcy had the flu and stayed home all day.

4   Lincoln Lake Camp meeting Cedar Springs 8 p.m. Darcy had to stay home. Had the flu yet.

5   Bostwick Lake 10:00 a.m. to 3:00 p.m. Cancelled Missionary meeting. Ice storm at night.

6   11:30—Darcy to Dr. Dodds. Went to Prayer Meeting. We all helped clean up the church. Chuck and Dar and Ron. All of us helped. Ate dinner at Mother & Dad's.

7   Ladies Work Meeting at Elsie Fuller's. I rode with Eva Curry. Went to TV Talent Spectacular. Chuck did real good. Dar stayed with Sherrie.

8   Cowbell Seed 4 bu, Vern and Al. 4165.60. Order oats, Gary $1.90. Went to G. R. and got 100 chairs for church and ate at Stage Coach. Darcy and Chuck worked at church. Sherrie got measles.

9   Darcy and Chuck worked at church at night. Ron and Ken went to YFC.

10   Had services in the new sanctuary. 155 in Sunday school. Went to rectors after church. Phyllis was home in afternoon for a while.

11   30° high. Dar was home sick. We drove to Joe Gless's. Dedee was here. Nancy came home from school. Darcy went to Deacon's Meeting. Ron and Ken went roller skating at G.R. and YFC.

12   Town Hall at 8 p.m. Drove to Joe Gless's. Stopped at bakery. I went to Ladies Missionary with Rita Johnson. Darcy went to Township Meeting.

13   7 p.m. Courtland Grange Hall. Went to Prayer Meeting. It was a business meeting. Voted to order pews and change

plans. Krauses were all here for supper. Looked at cars at Whittalls.

14   Ann got the car today. Ron 11 a.m. Dr. Chamberlain. Ron went to the dentist. Grandpa and Alma were here for the afternoon and Bill Horton. We all went to Ma and Dad's at night. Darcia stayed there.

15   Darcy took grist to Bill's for calf feed. Phyllis came home for the weekend. Darcia stayed.

16   Phyllis and I went shopping at Greenville. I got a new coat. Phyllis and Judy went to a game in G. R. Ron and Ken went to YFC. Ken stayed all night.

17   Went to church. 152 in S.S. The folks and Darcy's mother were here for dinner. Phyllis went back in afternoon. Darcia was at Dixie's.

18   Went to Greenville with Dedee for a coat. At night went to Norman's for Extension Meeting. Darcy went to Deacon's Meeting at church.

19   Alton called—they are coming out here now. Darcy went to Men's Fellowship.

20   Went to Prayer Meeting. Went to G.R. and bought paint for the bedroom.

21   1:30 p.m. Settlement Meeting Town Hall. Ann Krause helped me paint bedroom and bathroom. Went to Dedee's with Chuck and Dar. Darcy went with Aaron. Ron went swimming.

22   Bought Oliver tractor, scraper and loader. Went to G.R., Sparta and Greenville. Got new curtains for bedroom.

23   Phyllis came home at 11 a.m. She washed the kitchen for me. She and Judy went to YFC and so did Ron and Sue.

24   Went to church. Phyllis went back. Ron Pace and girlfriend and another couple were here at night. Also Betty Porter and Doris's children. 25Washed and ironed today. Went to G.R. with Darcy for tile. Darcy and Ron and Chuck worked at church.

26   Went to Marshall to Ronnie Gordon's funeral. Dedee and Aaron went with us and Darcy's Mother. At night we went to Holcomb's and to see Ma and Dad.

27   Went to Prayer Meeting. Went to Mrs. Rogans to a Deco Party. Ann Krause came and helped paint the hallway.

28   Scrubbed the kitchen floor with steel wool. Dedee was over. Darcy and Ron went to Ravenna to a cow auction.

29   Phyllis came home. I went to see Mother. Got groceries in afternoon. Darcy worked at church at night. Rained extra hard.

30   Elton's were here for supper. At night Crystal's, Reva's, Dedee's and family and Art and Ruth were here. Phyllis went to wedding. Ron went to YFC.

31   Alton's left at 7:45 a.m. for home. Went to church and Sunday school. Was to Roger's after church at night. Ron went to Ken K. in afternoon. Phyllis went back in afternoon.

April

1   Did washing. We all stayed home at night. Ron and Chuck and Darcia went to school. Voted!

2   Con Con passed! 8 p.m. North Park, Lincoln Lake Meeting. Darcy and Rev. Adams went. I saw Mrs. Rogan and Mrytle Rogers. Went to Missionary Meeting at night. Mrs. Hopper spoke. Darcy and I went to Rockford in morning. Darcy went to Dr. Ingland.

3   8 p.m. Township Board Meeting. Went to Prayer Meeting. Darcy and the kids. I stayed home with my sore back. Went to Dr. at Sparta.

4   Ron went to Easter concert at RHS. The men pulled in to start our new barn.

5   Uncle Gary's coming for supper. Ron brought a red convertible home to look at and took it back.

6   Worked all day. Planted first field of oats on Alma's. Had bulldozing too. Went to Lakes Fun Night with Chuck and Darcia. Ron and Sue went to YFC.

7   Went to Sunday school and church. 166 in S.S. Doug White came home with Chuck. Whites came for lunch after church.

8   Sowed oats on Holland Farm. Darcy and Royce Hammer went calling.

9   Plowed at Dad's yesterday. Darcy went to Men's Fellowship work meeting. I took Chuck and Dar skating with Grace Bible Church group.

10   Plowed and dragged at Dad's. Took Dar to the dentist. We all ate at Ma's. Phyllis came home. Went to Prayer Meeting at night.

11   Phyllis and Darcy's Mother and Darcia and I went to Robert Hall's shopping. At night Darcy and I drove over to Doris

and Mart's. Phyllis went to Cedar to Home Show. Ron went to Sue's. Chuck stayed at Ma's and Darcia to Grandma Porter's.

12   Finished planting oats on Dad's. Ron and I went to Robert Hall's and he got a suit and clothes. Then went to Rockford and he got the '60 red convertible. We went to Sheridan to see Harold at the hospital. The kids went to Ma and Dad's. Dad got his cast off.

13   Cold and sunny. Colored eggs today. Put fertilizer on hayfields on Holland Farm and Trumble Farm.

14   Easter. Went to church. Ma and Dad were here for dinner. Sue went to church at night and was here for lunch.

15   Phyllis went to town. Took me to Greenville to Dr. Olson's. Darcy went to work meeting at night at church. Also Phyllis, Judy, Chuck and Darcia.

16   Phyllis drove to WOOD. Didn't get a job. Judy and Janice were here at night.

17   Went to Prayer Meeting. Ken came and saw Ron afterwards. Phyllis went back.

18   Darcy and I drove to Lansing for cow drinkers (automatic drinking cups). Had dinner at Stage Coach.

19   Went to G.R. and saw Doris Dow. We all went to work meeting. Kenny came for supper and saw Ron. They worked on cars.

20   Chuck went to a birthday party at Bostwick Lake. Saw Ma and Gaylord's. Darcia went to Pioneer Girls. Had a hike. Darcy and Ron laid water pipe for new barn.

21   Went to church morning and night. Dedee and Aaron came at night after church.

22   Finished the barn. Darcy went to Deacon's Meeting. Took kids to 4-H Meeting.

23   Snowed. Got drinker at Tractor Supply. Heard Gerald Williams died. Had Helen Ingraham with me.

24   Had Helen and Brian. Went to Prayer Meeting.

25   Went to Gerald Williams's funeral, 750 attended. Mother and Dad came for the evening. Royce and Ron played catch. Called Phyllis two times.

26   Took Chuck for his lesson. Went to Teachers' Conferences for Chuck and Darcia. Sue came at night.

27   Went to school and helped serve for chicken Barbecue. Stayed for program. Phyllis interviewed at Cedar Springs.

28   Had my (Sunday school) girls home for dinner. Went to Art Gallery in afternoon. Sue went to church with Ron. Judy was here for dinner too.

29   Phyllis and I drove to G.R. She looked into job prospects. Had lunch at Smiths. Darcy went to work meeting. I went to Extension Meeting at Gould's.

30   Snowed hard. Drove Phyllis to G.R. to be interviewed at Wyoming school. She went back this afternoon. Darcy and Chuck went to work meeting at church.

May

1   Went to Prayer Meeting.

2   Called on Doris Dow. Went to Dr. Ingland. Got groceries at Cedar Springs. Dad and Darcy went to a Wheat Meeting. Mother stayed here.

3   Called on Edith. Took Chuck for lesson. Went to work meeting at church. Sherrie stayed all night. Ron went to Miracle Mart.

4   Plowed garden today. Went to Greenville. Ron went to YFC. Ron plowed for corn.

5   Went to church at night. Ron and Sue were here and Roger's. We went in afternoon to see Art and Ruth.

6   (No entry)

7   Lincoln Lake Board Meeting at camp.

8   Went to Prayer Meeting. Opening day for trial of driver of Joe Piatt's accident.

9   Ron went to Young Peoples party at Bub and Joyce's. Darcy went to work meeting. I went to the Folks.

10   Real big rain. We drove to Grand Rapids and looked at pianos. Bought one at Greenville. Had it delivered too. Gaylord got the old one. Went to work meeting at night. Ron and Sue went shopping.

11   Plowed and planted corn today. Went to Bob and Anna's.

12   Went to church. Sue and Ron were here after church.

13   (No entry.)

14   Called Phyllis about job appointment.

15   Drove to Mt. Pleasant and got Phyllis. She stayed overnight.

16   Took Phyllis to G.R. for interview at Radio Bible Class. She got the job. Starts June 10. Got a ticket. Took Phyllis back. Dorothy Nelson rode with me.

17   Drove to G.R. Had to pay $10 fine. Took a load of kids to Rainbow Lake. Darcia rode with Dedee and Aaron. Ron went to Sue's.

18   Got a load from Rainbow Lake. Darcia won a Bible and two awards. Went to Jack S. wedding in Cedar. Chuck and Dar stayed to Mother and Dad's.

19   Went to church. Crystal's came and Betty Porter and Doris and Mart. Sue was here for the evening and church.

20   Finished plowing and planting for corn at Folks. All done. Ron stayed out of school. Chuck played ball. Hit 2-baser. I went to church Business Meeting and Extension afterwards at Betty Patterson's.

21   Rained and real cold. Darcy planted Lyle's corn. Zelma and Gomer stopped in. I got a permanent at Dodgson's. Ron and I did his announcements. Darcy and Chuck went to church work meeting.

22   Went to Cedar to commencement. Had a party after for Kathy Adams.

23   Went to ballgame. Oakfield played Methodist Church. They won.

24   Got groceries at Cedar. Sugar prices jumped to $1.75 for 10 lbs. Went to church Work meeting. Phyllis called last night.

25   Went mushrooming with Crystal and Harold. Found a lot on Holland Farm. Ron and Sue went to YFC.

26   Went to church. In afternoon saw Mart and Doris. Bidstrups were here after church. Ron and Sue went to Holland with Janice and Royce.

27   Went to Phyllis's Swing Out and Class Night. Got home at 11:30. Darcy's mother went too. Had lunch after at Phyllis's. Everything was real nice.

28   Went to church. Dr. Welch had program. Dar was home sick. Ron and Chuck each had a ball game.

29   Went to G.R. and got Phyllis's cedar chest. Picked out Ron's watch. Rogers were here at night.

30   Went to Lincoln Lake for picnic. Darcy's mother was with us. At night Doris and Mart and My Folks were here. The kids went swimming.

31   Darcy and Chuck went to work meeting. I got groceries at night at Cedar. Stopped at Ma and Dad's.

June

1   Worked during the day. Went and got my hair fixed. Went to see Dave Becker in the hospital.

2   Went to church. Took lunch and ate at Crystal. Went to Phyllis's graduation. Was real nice. Went to Ron's Baccalaureate at night. Were all over to Dedee and Aaron's afterwards.

3   Drain Commission for Beaver Dam. Had graduation party at church. Was real nice. Phyllis drove home for it.

4   Lincoln Lake Board Meeting, 8 p.m. went to Ladies Missionary at night.

5   Phyllis came home. Was busy getting ready for party. Phyllis and I went shopping in G.R. for dresses. Went to Prayer Meeting. Mr. Hopper spoke.

6   Ron graduated today. Had a party afterwards. Was real nice. Lot came. He and Sue went to all-night party afterwards.

7   The kids went and saw Oakfield play Rockford Baptist. Oakfield won. Hauled a lot of hay today.

8   Hayed all day. Finished on Trumbull Farm. Baled on Whites. Went swimming to Lincoln Lake at night.

9   Went to Sunday school and church. Real bad storm. Tornado at Belmont. Ron and Sue and Paul and Phyllis and Mrs. Curry were all here at night.

10   Phyllis started work at Radio Bible Class today. She really likes it. Darcy and Ron and Phyl went to G.R. to look for cars.

11   Chuck had ball game at Townsend Park. They won. Darcy and I went. Phyllis and I went to Greenville to Jeff Branch's.

12   Went to Prayer Meeting. Phyllis ordered a car from Beckett.

13   Hayed all day. Chuck had game at Lakes. Ron did at Rockford. Oakfield beat Calvary. Ron did best he ever did.

14   Have well trouble. Went to Bible School Program. Had 256 out last day.

15   Hayed all day. Phyllis and Dar and I went to Greenville for Father's Day presents. Reva and Phil and Darcy's mother came at night. A real hard day.

16   Father's Day. Went to Sunday school and church. Had dinner at Ma and Dad's. Ron and Ken helped Carlton with Junior Church.

17   Mr. Adams took our pickup to Lansing. Kathy rode with Phyllis

18   We all went to church Work Meeting to get ready for the wedding.

19   Went to Prayer Meeting. Ray Curry Jr. spoke. Had tornado warning.

20   Went to Chuck's ball game, then to Ron's later. Both teams won.

21   Helped at church for wedding. Marilyn had a real nice wedding.

22   Had a picnic supper in yard. Darcy baled hay for Mart and Doris. Went to Meijer's shopping by Miracle Mart. Darcia and Phyllis got their hair cut. Gave Dar a permanent.

23   Went to church. Went and saw Art and Sue and Creeks in afternoon. Had farewell party for Rogers after. Nice get together.

24   Darcy baled hay for Bill Horton. Chuck's recital was today.

25   (No entry)

26   Phyllis got her car ('63 Dodge Dart). Went to Prayer Meeting. Had dinner with Mother for her birthday. Jessups were here

for supper. Rogers and Royce Hammer were here, and we made ice cream.

27   Went to Chuck's game. They lost. Went to Ron's game with Alpine. Oakfield won.

28   Stayed home tonight. Went to Meijer's at Greenville and got groceries.

29   Rogers moved today. Darcy and Ron helped load up. Jack and Bea (Hough) were here for supper.

30   Went to church morning and night. Ron went to Ken's for dinner.

July

1   Went to town to Stadium and Miracle Mart. Chuck and Dar went too. Went to Ladies Missionary. Darcy took Chuck and Dar to 4-H Meeting.

2   Had church ball practice at Wabasis. Dar and I went to Zoe's and saw pictures. Oakfield played Nevin's Lake and won. Went and saw Mart Holmden and Mrs. Dean at Funeral Home.

3   Went to town for groceries. Dedee and I went to Mrs. Dean's funeral. Just like a Catholic one. Went to Prayer Meeting.

4   Went to Rogers all day. Had dinner at Tunnel Park. Home made ice cream at night. Rode dune scooters.

5   Started hauling water to young cattle. Real dry. Judy came and stayed with Phyllis. They went to Lincoln Lake.

6   Rogers were here for dinner. Got groceries in afternoon. Phyllis went home with Judy. Ron and Ken went to the races.

7   Went to church both times. Went to Piatt's after church. Went to Beckers for 25th anniversary. Called on Whites and Aunt Alma and Uncle Herbert.

8   Ken S. came to stay with Chuck. Dar went to camp.

9   Went to Doris and Mart's at night. Phyllis rode horse. Darcy went to Men's Fellowship. Ron went to Uncle Gary's and Miracle Mart.

10   Went to camp and got Dar and Sharon. Chuck and Kenny stayed up. Went to Prayer Meeting. Ron helped Doris and Mart haul hay.

11   Finished Mart's hay. Broke baler and mower. Had grass fire and called Fire Department. Dar and Sharon went back to camp. Went to ballgame at Rockford. Oakfield vs. Rockford.

12   Judy came home with Phyllis. Oakfield boys played Cannonsburg. Won 10-9. Ron went to Miracle Mart and Uncle Gary's.

13   Went to Greenville shopping. At night went to Cedar Springs. Phyllis had some girls here. Ron and Ken went away.

14   Went to church and to Ma and Dad's after at night. Ron and Ken went to Allegan to church in morning. Phyllis and Judy went to Cadillac to reunion.

15   Took Chuck to camp. Boys' team beat Oaklawn. Ma was up and went too. Took Darcia to 4-H Meeting.

16   Finished a field of hay on Trumble farm. Ballgame. Men played Methodist church. Lost by one point. Phyllis got a permanent.

17   Wednesday went to see Chuck at camp at night. Terry Sheldon rode with us.

18   Had shower at church for Jack and Marilyn. Started combining today east of house. Ron took load of wheat in to Bill's at night.

19   Went to G.R. Had dinner at Lannings. Ron and Dar were with us. Phyllis left on her trip. Uncle Gary and Aunt Emily were here. Went to Ravanna for parts.

20   Finished hay at Trumbull's. Did little combining. Had to quit early. Lyle and Bart helped. Went to Cedar Springs at night.

21   Went to church. Saw Erwin and Beatrice and Zelma and Gomer in the afternoon.

22   Combined wheat today. First load tested 15.2. I took it in. Ron and Lyle took truck in at night. Darcy went to Deacon's Meeting.

23   Combined again today. Started at noon. Ron took truckload in today. Got home at 10:15 p.m. Lyle and Chuck went. Phyllis gave me a permanent.

24   Combined wheat again today. Phyllis worked at Bill's. Ron and Lyle baled straw.

25   Combined wheat. Real dry. Kids showed calves all day at Lowell. Dar got 4th out of 11. Chuck got 2nd out of 21. Went to ballgame. Oakfield beat Knapp Reformed.

26   Got wheat combining almost done. Broke belt on baler. Went to Ravanna for combine parts. Phyllis worked at Bill's. Ron drove load in.

27   Phyllis worked all day at Bill's. Finished wheat combining. Did a bin of oats for feed. Nicholsons were here at noon. We went swimming at Lincoln Lake at night. Dar came home from camp.

28   Ma and Dad and Darcy's mother were here for dinner. Phyllis went to Marilyn's. They went to Smith's church. Ron went to Allegan. Dedee and Aaron were here for lunch after church.

29   6:15 p.m. at Oaklawn. I drove load of wheat in to Greenville. Phyllis worked at Bill's.

30   Started combining oats today at Alma's. Got truckload. Went to ballgame. Oakfield beat Rockford Baptist 13-3. Phyllis worked at Bill's.

31   Rained. Went to G.R. and bought tires at Montgomery Ward. Went to Prayer Meeting.

August

1   Had baby shower for Sheila. Darcy combined oats on Alma's.

2   Combined oats. Boys' team played Cannonsburg. They lost. Chuck stayed with Jon Krause all night.

3   Cleaned house. Phyllis went to Hootenanny with Uncle Gary's. Darcy combined oats on Holland farm. Went to Dave Becker's wedding.

4   Went to the Funeral Parlor for Art's Dad. Went to church. Ron Nicholson came for afternoon to see Ron. We were

invited to Newman's for lunch after church. Saw Ken and Donna.

5   Cattle got out. Blue Monday. Baler broke. Combine broke. Darcy combined oats at Ma and Dad's. Got a part at night from Ravanna. I went to Mr. Rosenberger's funeral and Darcy's mother.

6   Put young cattle back in. Sent to L.G.'s ordination. Boys lost to Cannonsburg 13-5. Men won from Greenville 15-0. Ron hit his first homerun.

7   Finished combining oats. Phyllis got a call for her job of teaching at North Muskegon. Went to Prayer Meeting. Jack (Hough) spoke and had party for Pastor Adams afterwards.

8   Bailed and hauled straw today. Took Jack and looked at Scouts. Was to Dedee's awhile. De Armmonts from Detroit were here with Ma at night.

9   Baled 2nd cutting on Holland farm. 4 loads, real good! Boys' game with Cedar—won. Went to all-Star at Rockford. They beat Michigan Bell.

10   Phyllis signed her (teacher) contract. Finished hay in morning. Had workday at Lincoln Lake. —in the cabins. We all went up for dinner. Gordon was here. Beatrice and Irwin were here for supper. Rogers stopped.

11   Went to church. Judy was here for the weekend. Ron and Phyllis traded cars.

12   Got calves out and scrubbed up for the Fair. Baled straw at Ma and Dad's. Went to Ladies' Missionary. Was on food committee. Rained at night.

13   Darcy and Ron hauled Angel and Emily to the Fair. Darcia was interviewed for her vegetable (garden). She got a blue ribbon.

14   Dar entered her flower. Got a B. Chuck and Dar were interviewed by judge for their calves. Each got a blue ribbon. Phyllis and I and kids went to the Horse Show at night.

15   Today was Dairy Day. Dar placed 2nd out of 28. Chuck 4th of 12. Were proud of them. Went to Dairy Program at night. Kids did real well.

16   Went back to Fair for premium money. Dar got $6 and Chuck $3. Ron went at night. We went to see Dad and Mother. Darcia stayed over night there.

17   Ron told me some bad news. My heart aches. Darcy brought the calves home. Phyllis is to Judy's. Ron went to stay at Ken's overnight.

18   Went to church. Ron and Ken were to Allegan. Bill and Iris were here after church. Saw Bidstrups in the afternoon.

19   Ron drove down to enlist in air force and brought papers home to sign. Went to Church Annual Meeting. Judy was here.

20   We signed papers for Ron today. He took his test. Went to ballgame. Rockford Methodist beat us 3-1 to win the tournament.

21   Did more hay on Holland farm. 5 loads. Went to Prayer Meeting. Ron took calf to Dad's.

22   Finished all 2nd cutting hay. Boys' team lost 9-8 to Oaklawn at their field. Stopped for treats at Ballard's afterwards.

23   *One month and 9 days until Chuck's birthday.* (Entry not Mother's handwriting.)

24   *4 months from today is Christmas Eve.* (Entry not Mother's handwriting.)

25   Jack and Bea were at church all day. Rogers here for dinner and supper. Jack and Bea for lunch afterwards.

26   Ron found out when he leaves. Tomorrow at 11:30. Had ball practice.

27   Ron left for Air Force today. We all drove him to the base. Won ball game at Cedar.

28   Went to Prayer Meeting. Mr. Curry spoke.

29   Ron called from Chicago airport. Got books today. Was to Erharts. Marilyn came.

30   Phyllis and Marilyn went to Charlevoix. Sherrie came.

31   Went and saw Jack and Bea at night. Then on to Miracle Mart later at 9:30. Phyllis came home at 3:00 a.m.

September

1   Mr. Bopp spoke. Was real good. Had dinner at Ma and Dad's. Was to Bidstrups after church. Marilyn stayed all weekend.

2   Labor Day. Went to Dedee's and Aaron's for dinner. Was too cold for picnic, had rain. Jon Krause stayed.

3   Went to Cedar and got groceries. Went to Ladies Missionary. Rita rode with me.

4   Enrolled Chuck and Dar in school. Ingraham kids were here. Went to Prayer Meeting. Darcy went to Township Meeting. Phyllis called home.

5   Children had first day at school. Darcy cut hay. Got first letter from Ron. One paragraph long. Sounded all in.

6   Darcy and I baled three loads and a truckload of hay. Phyllis came home for the Weekend. Phyllis, Dar and I drove to Rockford at night.

7   Stayed home all day. Phyllis got her car checked and went to Cedar. Also saw Ann at night.

8   Went to church both times. Phyllis left at 5 to go back. Went at night too.

9   Darcy and I baled five loads of hay today. All done now. Stayed home at night.

10   Went to G.R. and Darcy got a new suit and topcoat. Ate at Sun Sai Gai. Had good time. Darcy went to Men's Fellowship.

11   Got nice letter from Ron. Went to Prayer Meeting at night. Went to Greenville in afternoon.

12   Went to Teachers Meeting at night. Chuck and Dar went too. Lots of rain today.

13   Poured more cement by barn. Took kids and had supper at McDonald's. Got Darcy's suit. Went shopping downtown and ended at Stadium. Got two dresses.

14   Phyllis came home today. Went shopping to Greenville. Dar sold her gourds. Judy Rogers was here for supper and Tammy. Myrtle was here awhile too.

15   Went to church. Phyllis left in afternoon. Had heifer bloat and die. Darcy bled her and Marhofers came. Cow got bloated too. Vet helped her. Dedee and Aaron were here for lunch afterwards.

16   Started silo filling today. Had four for dinner. Everyone was tired, and we went to bed early.

17   Filled silo, finished by noon. Glen Horton died today. 8 p.m. meeting at Lincoln Lake Camp.

18   Darcy's mother's birthday. Went to Prayer Meeting then on to funeral home afterwards. Darcy's mother was here all day for her birthday. Dedee and Aaron were here for supper. Finished silos.

19   Went to the funeral at church. Darcy and Elton went calling at night. Rained real hard.

20   Went to football game at Lowell. We won 6-0. Linda's boyfriend got hurt. Sat by Dedee's and Ingrahams.

21   Went to town and got polio vaccine. Took load to Youtharama. Stopped at McDonalds.

22   Went to church. Leareens came at night and for lunch afterwards.

23   Did washing. Went to Extension Meeting at Post's. Got home at 11:30. Offered to have next meeting at my house.

24   Stayed home at night. Was to Greenville during the day.

25   Went to Prayer Meeting. Went to GARB Meeting at Wealthy St. Church. Darcy took boys to Youtharama. Zoe was here after church.

26   5 days until Chuck's birthday. (Entry not Mother's handwriting.)

27   Bob and Anna DeBoer and children came for the evening.

28   Had slumber party for my class. 10 girls came. Went to bed at 3:30 am. Dar went to Sherrie's and Chuck to Ma and Dad's. Darcy and Elton went calling.

29   Went to church. Went to dinner at Dedee and Aaron's. Leereens came to church again. Ron called in afternoon.

30   Went to Rockford and Cedar. Stopped and drove new '63 red Dodge. Traded dressers last night with Ma for Darcia.

October

1   Ma and Dad and Phyllis and Gordon (Pratt) were here for supper. Chuck got 2 sweaters, 1 shirt, 4 dollars, and a model car.

2   Real bad rain storm with high winds. Drove to G.R. I went and got groceries and went to see Grandma Zeigenfuss. Went to prayer meeting at night and library. Darcy went to the Civic and heard Governor Romney speak on taxes. Called Phyllis at 11:00.

3   48°, cloudy and wet. Drove to Greenville and got mail order. Took Chuck and Dar over to Phyllis's to stay and visit school. We went through her school. Had supper on the way at Tastee Freeze at Cedar.

4   Rockford won Zeeland 27-0. Chuck and Dar visited school with Phyllis and went to football game. Jim and Beth Hough came and stayed over night. Phyllis and kids got home around 11.

5   Went to Red Flannel Day Parade. Jack and Bea were here at night a while. Made pizza at night.

6   Went to church. Drove by Wabasis Lake in afternoon. Also saw Dr. Hansen and was by his resort. Phyllis and Ruth left in afternoon. Newmans were here after church.

7   In 70's and sunny. Refilled tile silo today. Had silo fillers for dinner.

8   Darcy went to Men's Fellowship.

9   Darcy and I went to Roger's Plaza. Ate dinner at Howard Johnson's. Went to Prayer Meeting at night.

10   Went to Ladies Work Meeting all day. Varnished doors. Had sack lunch.

11   Went to Homecoming football game. Rockford 13-Sparta 13.

12   Dedee and I went to Greenville and to the library in afternoon. Chuck took a lesson. Stayed home at night. Ring the cow died today.

13   We went to church. Phyllis came home today. 4 new children went today with us.

14   Clare (Allen) and Darcy worked on crib and corn. Went to Dad's at night. Darcy put Antifreeze in Ron's car. Ron wrote—had sore throat.

15   Had sweet corn. Bob Kniseley was here for dinner. Went to town and got groceries and had car greased.

16   Phyllis came home tonight for Teachers' Institute. We all went to prayer meeting. Darcy and Elton went calling.

17   Mother got hit by car today. Has broken pelvis and chip of leg bone. At night I went to Well Child Annual Clinic Meeting at Horton School.

18   Phyllis went to Teachers' Meeting and saw Ma. I went to Greenville and Dar and I had our eyes tested. I got bifocals coming. Darcy went to Allandale to a meeting. Darcy and Ron got a hair cut. We all were home at night.

19   Rogers were here in afternoon. Phyllis got a permanent. Darcy and I and Chuck and Dar went and saw Ma at night.

20   Went to church. Phyllis and I and Dar went with Dad to see Ma. She wasn't keeping food down. Went to church at night. Phyllis went home after church.

21   Had extension Meeting. 13 were here. Darcy went with Dad to see Mother.

22   Took Darcy's mother to hospital to see Mother. Darcy went to Beacon Class Meeting at Anderson's.

23   Went to Dad's and saw Mabel Learson too. Went to Prayer Meeting. Darcy and Elton went calling after. Ethel came home with me.

24   Drove to see Mother. She was lots better. Went with Bea to Spring Lake Missionary Meeting.

25   Darcy and I took Dad and went to see Ma. Stopped and had coffee after with Dad. Gayla and Peggy went too.

26   Phyllis came at noon. Lincoln Lake work meeting. We were there for dinner. Phyllis went to young adult Halloween Party at Fuller's.

27   Went to Sunday school and church. Dad was here for dinner. Phyllis saw Ma and Marilyn in the afternoon. She left after church.

28   I went and saw Ma with Dad at night. Picked 4 loads of corn. Darcy bought 2 fresh heifers from Samricks.

29   Picked corn in morning. Darcy worked on cabin at Lincoln Lake. Dar went to Pioneer Girls.

30   Picked corn. Took Aunt Alma and Darcy's mother to see Mother. Went to Prayer Meeting at night. Darcy and Elton went calling.

31   Iris and I went calling. Rained most all day. Kids went Trick or Treating. Darcy took them.

November

1   Rockford beat Cedar 20-0. Picked corn. I went with Dad to see Mother. Darcy and kids went to football game. Froze and left 3rd quarter. Mrs. Leareen was saved today in her home.

2   Real cold and rainy. Picked corn. Phyllis and Ruth came home at noon. At night we went and saw Ma and stopped back at Miracle Mart. Chuck went too.

3   Went to church. Ron called home in morning. Phyllis left in afternoon. He called September 29 too.

4   Picked 8 loads of corn. Dorcas went with me to see Ma. Stopped at Miracle Mart and also in Rockford. Darcy went to Hastings for Lincoln Lake Board annual meeting with Pastor Adams.

5   Picked corn. Went and saw Crystal and Harold. Kids went to 4-H Meeting at Grange. I went to Ladies Missionary later. Got home after 11.

6   Alma and I went and saw Ma. Darcy's mother rode to see Ruth. Went to Prayer Meeting. Darcy had Township Meeting later.

7   Picked corn. Darcy went to Men's Fellowship. I went to Greenville in the morning.

8   Picked corn. Went to Greenville in morning. Dad was here for supper. We all went and saw Ma. Took Darcia to Grandma Porter's.

9   Picked corn. Moved elevator to Alma's barn. Went to Bronkema's open house at night. Rogers were here for supper.

10   Went to church. 162 in Sunday school. Phyllis stopped with 3 girls in afternoon. Went to church at night too. Men had meeting afterwards.

11   Darcy picked corn. I went to see Mother alone this afternoon. She wasn't feeling too good.

12   Picked corn. Went to Dar's Teacher Conference. Got real good report of her. Stayed home at night. Dar went to Pioneer Girls.

13   Picked corn on Alma's. Almost done. Took Darcy's mother to see Mother. Went to Prayer Meeting at night.

14   Darcy picked corn. Went to Ladies Work Meeting. Packed 8 boxes of cookies to send (to servicemen). Stayed home at night.

15   Moved to Dad's today and started picking corn. Went and saw Mother at night. Chuck went to his Grandma Porter's.

16   Picked 9 loads of corn at Dad's. Broke wagon. Chuck and Dar went to 4-H Hayride. I cleaned Mother's house. We ate dinner there. Heard Phyllis was in a car accident.

17   Bad thunderstorm at night. Ron called today to tell Darcy, Happy Birthday a week ahead. Went to church. Dedee and Aaron's were here for lunch at night.

18   Went and saw Mother today. She was a little better. Took out Aunt Austa. Ron wrote and sent $60 home. Dad was here at night.

19   Went to Extension Meeting at Ethel Williams.

20   Got the flu today. Couldn't see Mother. Darcy and kids went to Prayer Meeting.

21   Still have flu. Layed in bed all day.

22   **President Kennedy was assassinated today**. Watched TV all day. Still have flu. Darcy worked.

23   *Father's birthday. Good boy's birthday.* (Not Mother's handwriting) Phyllis came home. Had birthday dinner at noon. Went to Bidstrups at night for spaghetti dinner. Phyllis and Darcia went to see Ma.

24   Stayed home. Darcy and kids went to church. Phyllis was home for long weekend.

25   No school today as it was Kennedy's funeral. Phyllis and I went to see Ma in afternoon. She's not so good. Phyllis left at 6:00. Lyle disked.

26   Was home all day today. Kids went back to school. Clare Allen came and went back to disking.

27   Went and saw Ma in afternoon. Stopped and got groceries at Meijer's. Went to Thanksgiving supper at church. Phyllis came home for Holiday.

28   Thanksgiving. Went to Grandpa and Alma's for Thanksgiving. Had turkey. Watched TV at night.

29   Phyl and Dar went to Greenville to Dr. Olson. Finished all the disking today and put it up. Phyllis and I and Dar went and saw Ma. Also went and saw new airport. Shopped at Arlan's on the way home.

30   Chuck is sick yet. Zelma and Gomer and his niece and nephew came to see the farm and cows. Phyllis and Marilyn went to the Civic to a play at night.

December

1   Chuck stayed home all day. Dedee and Aaron went to church with us at night and came back for lunch. 175 in Sunday school today. Phyllis went back at night at 9:30. Hammers were in church both times today.

2   Jack and Bea were here. Went to Cedar and ordered Scout. Went to see Ma. She wasn't good at all today. Stopped and got groceries at Meijer's. Ron wrote today. Stayed home at night.

3   Darcy and I went to Greenville in afternoon. Brian arrived in Muskegon at 4:30 to see Phyllis.

4   I went at noon to stay with Mother, and we picked out Christmas gifts for all the grandchildren. Tiffanys were here

for supper and spoke at prayer meeting. Darcy helped put up tables later.

5   Men's Banquet was today. I helped in afternoon. Phyllis and Brian came home and they went too. Brian is a very nice fellow. The banquet was nice—a good turn out.

6   Beautiful day today. Brian and Phyllis and Darcy and I went to the hospital to see Mother. She wasn't feeling too good yet. Ate at the Stagecoach. We all stayed home at night. We brought Ron's car home.

7   Brian and Phyl went to Greenville. We were all home for night and watched TV. Dad came for supper.

8   We all went to church. Dedee and Aaron came at night and we all watched slides. Reva and Phil and Darcy's mother were here in the afternoon.

9   Phyllis and Brian left at 7 for Muskegon. I went and saw Ma in afternoon. We all stayed home at night.

10   *Mother's birthday. Good good girl's birthday.* (Not Mother's handwriting) Got watch from Darcy and Phyllis. Calendar from Chuck. Apron from Dar. Card with money from Ron. Roses from the Folks. Bea spoke at Ladies Missionary.

11   Mother dangled (her feet) for the first time today. Darcy and I went to G.R. He went to Telefarm Meeting. I spent 3 hours with Ma. We ate at McDonald's. Went to Prayer Meeting at night.

12   *Phyllis's birthday. Good girl's birthday.* (Not Mother's handwriting) Typed parts for my class and delivered them in snowstorm. Got order from Sears.

13   Today was Phyllis's birthday. Baked a cake and she couldn't come home. Had to take debate kids to G.R. tomorrow. I

went and saw Ma. We were all home at night. Real stormy. Bad wind and snow.

14   Went to Greenville for order. Chuck and I. Darcy had Tom and Jr. help fix barn. Kids and I went to Rockford and mailed Ron's Christmas box. Real cold and snowy out. Gave Dar a permanent.

15   Went to church and Sunday school. Chuck was to Krause's and Dar to Moon's. Darcy's mother was here for dinner.

16   Zero. Darcy and I went to G.R. and saw Mother. She was going to be moved. Went to Extension Christmas supper at Langston. Had chicken supper. Was real good.

17   Zero weather. Stayed home all day. Did ironing. Heard from Ron. Mother was moved to Mary Free Bed.

18   Zero. Went and saw Mother at Mary Free Bed. Went to Prayer Meeting at night.

19   Zero. Stayed home all day. Chuck and Dar had Christmas party at school. Played Old Maid with the kids. Jack Hough came with Scout. (Dad and Mother bought this for them to take to Peru.)

20   *Last day of school until next year.* (Not Mother's handwriting) Today is our wedding anniversary. Went to Chinese restaurant. Brought pizza home later. Phyllis came home. Judy came too.

21   Zero. Went to Greenville shopping. Phyllis and Judy took Chuck and Dar to Wurzburg. Darcy and I went with Dad to see Ma. Dad was here for supper.

22   Christmas Program today. Turned out real good. Practiced in afternoon with my class. Had good attendance.

23   Darcy and I went to Cedar for turkey. Stopped and saw his mother. Phyllis and I and Mrs. Visser went to see Ma. She was feeling good. Got a letter from Brian.

24   Had a nice Christmas Eve. Went to town to Rockford for last minute shopping. Ron called while we were opening presents. Stayed up late and watched TV.

25   Had a nice Christmas. Dad was here for dinner. Had turkey. We all went down and saw Mother and took the kids down with presents. Watched TV at night.

26   Stayed home all day and at night watched TV. Crystal and Harold and Rose were here for supper. Had nice visit with them.

27   Darcy and Phyllis and I and Dar went to G.R. to P.C. (Production Credit) and on over to see Mother. It snowed real hard. Chuck was to Gordon's to play. Phyllis went to see Marilyn at night.

28   Was home all day. Diane came to play with Dar. Went to library with DeDee's. Went to Porter's Christmas get together at Legion Hall. 51 were there. Had real nice time.

29   Went to church both times. Hammers were here for lunch after church. Stayed until midnight. Had a real good time.

30   Phyllis and I went to see Ma. Had slumber party for my girls. 6 came. Went to bed at 3:30. Had barbecues and sundaes. Real noisy and good time.

31   New Year's Eve. Phyllis took the girls home for me. Dad was here in afternoon. I made biscuits for him and us. Phyllis got Marilyn.

About the Author

Phyllis Dolislager freelances as a writing consultant. She is an inspirational speaker, and she gives writing workshops.

For Christmas 2000, Phyllis wrote her memoir/testament, *A King-Size Bed, A Silk Tree & A Fry Pan,* for her family. Her Michigan family then requested a book about growing up on the farm in the 50's and 60's. Consequently, she is the author of the family memoir, *Lessons Learned on the Farm.* Her other books are available on www.byphyllis.com.

Phyllis and her husband Ron, Finance Director of World Mission Centre/Live School live in Townsend, Tennessee.

Printed in the United States
87861LV00003B/265-285/A

9 781931 232920